County Fair Blue Ribbon Winning Cookbook

Main Dish, Casserole, & Vegetable Recipes

Series 1

By Amber Richards

Table of Contents

Introduction	1
Main Dishes	3
Lasagna Mexican Style	3
Asparagus Beef Stir-Fry	4
Show Stopping Tomato Quiche	5
Tart Filled Prosciutto & Brie	6
Stuffed Shells with Chicken Alfredo	8
Potato Baskets & Chicken	9
Salmon with Fruit Salsa	10
Chicken Tenders with a Coconut Crust	11
Pork Medallions Country Inspired	11
Sweet and Sour Meatballs	12
Down Home Pork & Apples	13
Pork Chops with Tangy Fruit Sauce	14
Meatloaf Mania	15
Flank Steak Grilled Asian Style	16
Haddock Glazed with Cilantro Lime Butter	17
Rosemary & Honey Baked Chicken	17
Zucchini and Sausage Stir-Fry	18
Chicken Hand Pies with a Kick	18
Spiced Shrimp & Frozen Margarita	20
Rich Red Wine Sauce with Meatballs	21
Savory Meatball Pie	22
Chicken Manicotti Mexican Style	23
Penne Chicken & Gorgonzola Cheese	24
Macaroni & Pepper Jack Cheese	25
Steak Peppered & Port Cherry Sauce Topped	26
Spinach & Pepperoni Quiche	27
Cornish Hens with Pineapple Stuffing	28
Pizza Waffles	29
Macaroni and Cheese Supreme	29
Roasted Chicken with Lemon Sauce	30
Dumplings & Round Steak	32
Seafood Lasagna	33
Caribbean Pot Roast Slow Cooked	34

Tamale Pie Slow Cooked	35
Adobo-Lime Southwest Hash	36
Sausage Bake Southwest Style	37
Cheesy Spiced Chicken Bowl	38
Pork with Maple Ginger Sauce	39
Crab Spinach Chicken	40
Pulled Beef Sweet and Savory Dinner	41
Beef Brisket with a Tangy Twist	42
Onion & Turkey Bacon Spirals	43
Primavera A La Turkey	44
Chicken Piccata	45
Ultimate Lasagna	46
Vegetables & Salads	49
Coleslaw with Blueberries	49
Bread & Butter Banana Peppers	49
Grilled Chicken with Brown Rice Salad	50
Superb Corn Salad	51
Mandarin Broccoli Salad	51
Vegetable Lasagna	53
Fresh Cucumber & Tomato Salad	54
Bacon, Green Pea And Cashew Salad	55
Mushroom & Green Bean Pie	56
Veggie Sandwich Grilled	57
Mediterranean Vegetables Grilled	58
Mediterranean Pasta & Vegetables	58
Cheesy Carrots	59
Sweet Potatoes Delight	60
Spinach Salad	61
Cranberry & Sweet Potato Crepes	62
Egg Veggie Strata	64
Mustard Potato Salad	65
Orzo & Wild Rice Salad	65
Casseroles	67
Asparagus & Ham Casserole	67
Cheesy Polenta Casserole	68
Cheese and Scrambled Egg Casserole	69
Soups	71
Cheese Dumplings & Hearty Beef Stew	71
Homemade Barley & Chicken Soup	72
Chicken & Biscuit Soup	73
Creamy Cauliflower Soup	74

Cream of Parsnip Carrot Soup	75
Hearty Sausage Stew	76
Swiss Onion Soup	76
Pumpkin Curry Soup	77
Healthy & Delicious Root Soup	78
Bean & Ham Chowder	79
Goulash Hungarian Style	80
Spiced Shrimp Bisque	81
Beefy Mushroom Stew	81
Delicious Bean Soup	83
Chili Pepperoni Pizza Style	84
Sweet Bell Pepper Soup	84
Old Fashioned Bean Soup	85
Black Bean & Sweet Potato Chili	86
Pasta & Turkey Soup	87
Winter Hardy Beef Stew	88
Walnut & Blue Cheese Tart	91
Chicken Buffalo Dip	92
Blue Cheese Dip	92
Rhubarb Crepes	93
Chicken Salad with Curry Sandwiches	94
Soufflé Italian Style	94
Cheese Spread Louisiana Style	95
Special Chicken Salad	96
Beef & Onion au Jus	97
Corn Bread & Rhubarb Stuffing	98
Strawberry Crepes	98
Little Sausage Buns	100
Italian Sun-Dried Tomato Jam	101

Introduction

Whether you are looking for recipes to enter into your local county fair, or another cooking contest, or looking for a new family favorite, you will find some seriously amazing tasting recipes in this book.

All the recipes found here are at least blue ribbon winning recipes (1st place) or higher, such as Grand Champion or Best in Show winners.

This is the first of a series of cookbooks that will be released (all of them blue winning recipes), for cakes, cookies, pies, breads and other desserts. Collect them all to add to your recipe repertoire.

If you are wanting to make these recipes in a different unit of measure, here is a wonderful recipe converter tool, http://www.cooks.com/rec/convert/.

Abbreviation	Means
C or c	cup
lb	pound
oz	ounce
pt	pint
tsp or t	teaspoon
Tbsp or T or TB or Tbl	tablespoon

Enjoy exploring and making these amazing recipes!

Main Dishes

Lasagna Mexican Style

1-1/2 pounds ground beef
1/4 teaspoon garlic powder
1/4 teaspoon cayenne pepper
1 teaspoon salt or to taste
1-1/2 teaspoons ground cumin
1 tablespoon chili powder
1 teaspoon pepper or to taste
1 can (14-1/2 ounces) diced tomatoes, drained
10 to 12 corn tortillas
2 cups (16 ounces) small curd cottage cheese
1 cup shredded pepper Jack cheese
1 egg
1/2 cup shredded cheddar cheese
3 green onions, chopped
1/4 cup sliced ripe olives
2 cups shredded lettuce
1/2 cup chopped tomatoes

Instructions
Start with a large skillet, add the beef and let it cook over a medium heat. Then drain excess liquid, and add the spices, (cumin, cayenne, chili powder, garlic powder, salt, pepper) and tomatoes. Mix it up cook 10 minutes. Take out the tortillas and spread them across the bottom and sides of a greased 9X13 inch baking dish.

Now, it is time to add the beef mixture to the tortillas. Once this is done, set the tortillas aside for a few minutes. Combine together cottage cheese, Monterey Jack cheese and eggs then pour this mixture over the tortillas.

Place in the oven at 350° F. for about 30 minutes. Remove from heat, then sprinkle cheese, lettuce, tomatoes, green onions and olives in a decorative way across the top of the casserole for a dish that can serve eight people.

Asparagus Beef Stir-Fry

1 pound beef top round steak (3/4 inch thick)
2 tablespoons plus 1/2 cup water, divided
1/2 teaspoon salt
1/4 teaspoon pepper
2 tablespoons cornstarch
1/8 teaspoon hot pepper sauce
3 tablespoons canola oil, divided
2 cups fresh asparagus pieces or fresh broccoli florets
1 cup sliced cauliflower
1 small sweet red or green pepper, julienned
1 small onion, cut into 1/4-inch wedges
1 tablespoon ketchup
1 teaspoon red wine vinegar
2 teaspoons beef bouillon granules
1 tablespoon soy sauce
Hot cooked rice (enough for 6 servings)

Instructions
Cut the beef into three strips of 3 inch thickness. Put together cornstarch, water, salt, pepper and hot pepper sauce in a large plastic bag, then mix it up, and seal. Place half the beef in this bag and shake to coat.

Take the beef and fry it with 1 tablespoon of oil until it is fully cooked, and then allow it cool. Repeat with the other half of the beef.

Time to put the asparagus and the cauliflower together and sauté them for four minutes, until tender, yet crisp. Add the pepper and onion, then cook for a few minutes more. Place the beef back in the skillet with the vegetables.

County Fair Blue Ribbon Winning Cookbook

Mix the soy sauce, ketchup, bouillon, vinegar in a bowl, and add these to the skillet. Fire it up, and cook for two minutes until evening is hot. Serve over rice. This yields enough for 6 people.

Show Stopping Tomato Quiche

1/8 teaspoon pepper
1/3 cup shortening
3/4 cup flour
1/2 cup cornmeal
4 to 5 tablespoons cold water
1/2 teaspoon salt

FILLING:
1/2 teaspoon dried basil
2 cups chopped plum tomatoes
1 teaspoon salt
1/8 teaspoon pepper
1/2 cup chopped green onions
2 tablespoons all-purpose flour
2 eggs
1 cup evaporated milk
1/2 cup shredded cheddar cheese
1/2 cup shredded Swiss cheese

Instructions
Start by putting together the first 6 ingredients in a small bowl. Mix and shape it with a fork until it resembles a ball, and then chill it for about 30 minutes in a refrigerator.

On a lightly floured surface, roll out dough to fit a 9-in. pie pan; transfer pastry to pan. Trim to 1/2 in. beyond edge of plate; flute edges. Bake at 375° for 10 minutes. Cool completely.

Take the plum tomatoes and place them in the crust, and then add the salt, basil, pepper, onions and cheese. Put the flour, milk and eggs together in a small bowl, and whisk them. Pour this over the tomatoes in the pastry crust.

Bake it at 375°F until it gets completely cooked (about 30 minutes), that is when a knife is inserted in the center comes out clean. Allow to cool slightly and then serve. Makes 6-8 servings.

Tart Filled Prosciutto & Brie

2 teaspoons sugar
1/2 cup cold butter, cubed
1/2 cup finely chopped pecans
1-1/2 cups all-purpose flour
1 egg yolk
1 teaspoon Dijon mustard
1 tablespoon water

FILLING:
2 cups fresh baby spinach
3 shallots, thinly sliced
1 tablespoon olive oil
4 thin slices prosciutto or deli ham
3 eggs
2/3 cup milk
1/8 teaspoon crushed red pepper flakes
4 ounces Brie cheese, rind removed and cubed
1/4 teaspoon minced fresh thyme
1/4 teaspoon salt
1/8 teaspoon pepper
1/8 teaspoon ground nutmeg

Instructions
Heat the oven to 350° F. Chop the pecans in a food processor (or by hand), and then add the flour and sugar, continue to blend until everything is mixed. In a separate bowl, add egg yolk, water and

mustard and whisk them all together. Add this egg yolk mixture to the pecan mix to form a dough.

Put this dough into an ungreased 14x4-in. fluted tart pan, pressing it on to the bottom, and move the pressure sideways to get it on the sides as well. Put it in the oven, and bake until the crust is visibly browned (15-23 minutes), through only lightly. Remove from heat and let it cool.

Add the onions to a large skillet along with shallots and sauté them, then add the spinach and cook for two more minutes. Let this cool as well and set aside.

Use the same skillet and cook the proscuitto until it gets crisp. Drain. Put together eggs, milk and seasonings in a large bowl and start mixing. Pour the spinach mixture into the crust, after that the egg mixture needs to be added; and finally top with the cheese and proscuitto.

Bake again (about 30-35 minutes), until a knife put in at the center comes out clean, then sprinkle thyme on the top. Allow to cool slightly before cutting. It can serve up to 12 people.

Stuffed Shells with Chicken Alfredo

2 tablespoons olive oil, divided
1 package (12 ounces) jumbo pasta shells
1-1/2 pounds boneless skinless chicken breasts, cut into 1/2-inch cubes
1/2 pound sliced baby Portobello mushrooms
1 egg, lightly beaten
1 carton (15 ounces) ricotta cheese
3-1/4 cups grated Parmesan cheese, divided
1 cup (4 ounces) shredded mozzarella cheese
1 teaspoon dried parsley flakes
2 garlic cloves, minced
2 cups heavy whipping cream
3/4 teaspoon salt
1/2 teaspoon pepper
1/2 cup butter, cubed

Instructions
Follow directions on the package to cook the pasta, and cook the chicken in a large skillet. Let it cool. You may have some oil remaining in the pan you used to cook the chicken, use it to sauté the mushrooms. Let it cool.

Mix the ricotta, egg, parmesan (one part of it), mozzarella and seasonings together in a bowl.

Take a cooked pasta shell and stuff each piece with some of the cheese mixture. Place them in a greased baking dish, and then add in the chicken and mushrooms.

Sauté in a saucepan the butter, add garlic and cook for a minute. Add cream, continue cooking and then finally add the second portion of parmesan cheese. Continue cooking for about another minute.

County Fair Blue Ribbon Winning Cookbook

Pour this over the stuffed shells, chicken and mushrooms. It is time to bake this delicious combination at 350° for about 30 minutes, covered. Remove the cover, and continue baking for 5 more minutes. This makes 10 servings.

Potato Baskets & Chicken

4-1/2 cups frozen shredded hash brown potatoes, thawed
1-1/2 teaspoons salt
1/4 teaspoon pepper
6 tablespoons butter, melted

FILLING:
2 teaspoons chicken bouillon granules
1 teaspoon Worcestershire sauce
1/2 teaspoon dried basil
1/2 cup chopped onion
1/4 cup butter, cubed
1/4 cup all-purpose flour
2 cups milk
1 cup frozen peas, thawed
3 cups cubed cooked chicken

Instructions
Mix the butter, salt & pepper, and potatoes in a bowl. Divide this into 6 portions, then press these portions into 6 greased 10 oz. custard cups.

Sauté onions in a sauce pan along with melted butter. Then, pop in the bouillon, Worcestershire Sauce, flour and basil, stirring constantly. Pour in the milk and mix, then continue to cook for about two minutes. Add the green peas and chicken. Pour this batter into the custard cups.

Bake at 375° F for 30 minutes. This delicious meal serves 6 people.

Salmon with Fruit Salsa

Ingredients
4 salmon fillets (6 ounces each)
2 teaspoons finely chopped chipotle peppers in adobo sauce
1/4 teaspoon salt
2 tablespoons brown sugar
3 garlic cloves, minced

SALSA:
1 tablespoon minced fresh cilantro
1 tablespoon minced fresh mint
2 teaspoons olive oil
2 cups chopped fresh strawberries
2/3 cup chopped peeled mango
1/3 cup chopped red onion
2 tablespoons lime juice

Instructions
Mix together garlic, peppers, sugar, and salt then rub this spicy mixture over the salmon.

Moisten a paper towel with some oil. Grease the grill rack and place the salmon on the grill rack. Begin grilling at a high-temperature until the fish is done cooking. Usually this is indicated by a fork that is inserted into the thickest part, and turned slightly will flake easily. Roughly it should take about 5 minutes for each 1/2 inch of thickness.

Stir together the salsa ingredients, and serve with the salmon, making for a great dish that can serve four people.

County Fair Blue Ribbon Winning Cookbook

Chicken Tenders with a Coconut Crust

1 cup shredded coconut
1 cup Bisquick mix
3/4 teaspoon paprika
1/2 teaspoon salt
2 tablespoons Dijon mustard
1 tablespoon ground coriander
1/2 cup sweetened condensed milk
4 boneless chicken breasts, skinned and cut into strips
1/4 cup butter, melted

Instructions
Preheat a 350° F. oven. Mix the coconut, paprika, salt and Bisquick together in a bowl. In a separate bowl mix the milk, coriander and mustard. Dip the chicken in the milk wash first, then roll in the coconut mixture. You may want to press it a little to make sure the coconut sticks to the chicken.

Place the chicken in a greased baking dish and bake it with the butter for 35 minutes.
Delicious goodness that will leave you wanting for more. Makes 4-5 servings.

Pork Medallions Country Inspired

2 pork tenderloins (1 pound each)
6 tablespoons butter, divided
3/4 pound small fresh mushrooms
2 small apples, cored and cut into rings
2 small onions, sliced and separated into rings

APPLE CREAM SAUCE:
1 package (8 ounces) cream cheese, cubed
1 cup apple cider or juice

1/4 cup apple brandy or additional apple cider
1 teaspoon dried basil

Instructions
Slice pork into two pieces 1/2 inch thick. Flatten that down until it reaches ¼ inch. Cook the pork with butter until it is cooked through. Remove from heat, but make sure that it stays warm.

Using the same skillet add apple, mushrooms, and onions and sauté them for a few minutes. Place these sautéed items over the pork.

Heat the cream cheese and cider in the skillet and cook for a few minutes until the cheese is melted. Add brandy and basil then continue cooking. Add the pork and the sautéed vegetables, and heat until everything is hot. Makes 6 servings.

Sweet and Sour Meatballs

2 medium carrots, julienned
1 small onion, halved and sliced
2 pounds frozen fully cooked home-style meatballs, thawed (or cook your own)
1 garlic clove, minced
1 small green pepper, julienned
4-1/2 teaspoons soy sauce
1 jar (10 ounces) sweet-and-sour sauce
Hot cooked rice

Instructions
In a 3 quart microwavable dish, put the meatballs inside and add garlic, pepper, onion and carrots.

In a separate bowl, mix soy sauce and sweet and sour sauce, then pour over the above ingredients. Cover and microwave on high 7-8 minutes, until the veggies are tender. Stir twice during the heating process, and make sure the meatballs are hot. Serve over cooked rice. Makes 8 servings.

Down Home Pork & Apples

3 pounds boneless pork, cut into 1-inch cubes
3/4 cup all-purpose flour
1 pound sliced bacon, cut into 2-inch pieces
3 medium onions, chopped
Vegetable oil, optional
3 medium tart apples, peeled and chopped
1 teaspoon rubbed sage
1/2 teaspoon ground nutmeg
1 teaspoon salt
1/4 teaspoon pepper
1/2 cup water
1 cup apple cider
4 medium potatoes, peeled and cubed
5 tablespoons butter, divided
Additional salt and pepper
1/2 cup milk
 Minced fresh parsley, optional

Instructions

Cook bacon in a skillet until it is crisp, then put on paper towels to drain excess grease. Sauté onions in the bacon grease until soft, then remove the onions with a fork and set aside. Roll the pork in flour and cook in the pan drippings, if you need to add extra oil during this phase, that's fine. When pork is thoroughly cooked, remove from heat.

Add the onions, apples, bacon, sage, nutmeg, salt and pepper to the pork. Mix in with water and cider. Bake it for 2 hours at 325° F. covered.

Boil the potatoes in water in a saucepan. After boiling, reduce heat and cook for 15 minutes until they are soft. Drain and add butter, salt & pepper and milk, and then mash. Place these mashed potatoes on top of the pork.

Melt a little butter and brush on the mashed potatoes. Broil for 5 minutes until browned, 6 inches from the heat. Garnish with parsley, makes 10 servings.

Pork Chops with Tangy Fruit Sauce

1 tablespoon canola oil
1 can (10-3/4 ounces) condensed chicken broth, undiluted
4 pork chops, about 1 inch thick
2 tablespoons brown sugar
2 tablespoons cornstarch
1 teaspoon ground ginger2 tablespoons soy sauce
1 tablespoon vinegar
1/2 cup apple juice
1 large apple, coarsely chopped
Cooked rice
Sliced green onions

Instructions
Heat oil in a large skillet, and brown the pork chops. Add in the vinegar, soy sauce, and chicken broth and mix, and bring the mixture to a boil. Reduce the heat, and let it simmer for a few minutes, until chops are completely cooked. Remove from heat, yet keep the pork chops warm.

In a small bowl mix cornstarch, ginger, apple juice and brown sugar. Turn skillet up to medium and pour this in, add the apple and cook until it is tender and the liquid has thickened.

Serve the pork chops over cooked, hot rice then pour the fruit sauce over the top. Garnish with some green onions. Makes 4 servings.

County Fair Blue Ribbon Winning Cookbook

Meatloaf Mania

1 medium onion, peeled and cut into eighths
2 garlic cloves
2 ribs celery, cut into 2-inch pieces
4 slices white bread, torn into pieces
2 ½ pounds ground beef
2 carrots, peeled and cut into 2-inch pieces
½ cup fresh flat-leaf parsley
1 large egg
¾ cup ketchup (divided)
1 tablespoon coarse salt
2 teaspoons freshly ground pepper
2 tablespoons packed brown sugar
2 teaspoons dry mustard
2 tablespoons finely chopped red, green and yellow bell peppers

Instructions
Preheat oven to 350° F. In a food processor, process bread until fine crumbs are made. Add this and beef to a separate bowl.

Back to the food processor, chop garlic, carrots, onions, celery and parsley until fine. Add to the beef mixture. Then add 1/2 the ketchup, spices and the egg, then mix with your hands until thoroughly blended. Put in a 5X9 greased loaf pan.

Pour remaining ketchup, brown sugar and mustard into a bowl, then brush on the meatloaf.

Bake about 1 1/2 hours, until a meat thermometer inserted into the middle reads 160°F. If the top is getting too dark during the cook time, cover it with foil. When done, remove from heat and allow to set for 15 minutes before serving. Serves 8 people.

Amber Richards

Flank Steak Grilled Asian Style

1 teaspoon Chinese five-spice powder
1 teaspoon minced garlic
1/2 teaspoon minced gingerroot
1/4 c. Worcestershire sauce
1/4 c. soy sauce
3 T. honey
1 T. sesame oil
1 beef flank steak (1-1/2 pounds)
2 T. hoisin sauce
1 T. sesame toasted seeds
3 green onions, thinly sliced

Instructions
You need to start by putting together the first seven ingredients in a large plastic bag, preferably one that is resealable. Next, pop in the steak, seal the bag and put it in the refrigerator for the night.

When ready to cook, drain the marinade and grill steaks over medium heat to your desired done-ness. Remove from heat.

Allow it to cool for a few minutes, then slice it up and splash some hoisin sauce on it. If you want, you can add a few sesame seeds and garnish with onions. This dish is suitable for serving six people.

County Fair Blue Ribbon Winning Cookbook

Haddock Glazed with Cilantro Lime Butter

4 haddock fillets (6 ounces each)
1/2 teaspoon salt
1/4 teaspoon pepper
1 tablespoon lime juice
1 teaspoon grated lime peel
3 tablespoons butter, melted
2 tablespoons minced fresh cilantro

Instructions
Preheat broiler. Now that the broiler is chugging along in the background, season the fillets with some salt and pepper, and when done, put in the oven and broil until the fish can be easily flaked with a fork.

Mix the remaining ingredients in a bowl and serve this mixture over the haddock. Serves 4 people.

Rosemary & Honey Baked Chicken

1/4 cup balsamic vinegar
1/4 cup minced fresh rosemary
1/4 cup honey
2 tablespoons olive oil
1 teaspoon salt
1/4 teaspoon pepper
6 bone-in skinless chicken breast halves (7 ounces each)

Instructions
Mix oil, rosemary, honey and vinegar in a small bowl, placing half this marinade into a large re-sealable plastic bag. Add the chicken, turn to coat and chill at least 2 hours in the refrigerator. Cover and chill the other half of the marinade as well.

Amber Richards

When ready to cook, drain the marinade from the chicken and toss it out. Put chicken in a 9X13 baking pan, then add salt & pepper. Bake at 350° F. uncovered for 1 hour. Baste during cooking with reserved marinade. Makes 6 servings.

Zucchini and Sausage Stir-Fry

4 cups julienned or shredded zucchini
2 cups seeded chopped tomatoes
1 pound mild Italian sausage links, cut into 1/4-inch slices
1/2 cup chopped onion
1/4 teaspoon dried oregano
1/4 teaspoon hot pepper sauce
1 teaspoon lemon juice
1/4 teaspoon salt
Grated Parmesan cheese

Instructions
Cook onion and sausage in a large skillet until it is thoroughly cooked. Then add the tomatoes, lemon juice, oregano, pepper sauce and zucchini and cook for 5 minutes, uncovered. Top with cheese before serving. Serves 4 people.

Chicken Hand Pies with a Kick

Dough:
1 teaspoon curry powder
1/8 teaspoon cayenne pepper
3 cups Bisquick mix
2/3 cup very warm water (120-130 degrees F)

Filling:

1 tablespoon seeded and minced jalapeno
1 clove garlic, minced

County Fair Blue Ribbon Winning Cookbook

2 tablespoons cooking oil
1 cup chopped yellow onion
1 tablespoon unbleached all-purpose flour
2 teaspoons curry powder
1/4 teaspoon allspice
2 tablespoons water
2 tablespoons tomato paste
1 small cooked chicken (skinned, de-boned, and chopped)

Topping:

1 egg, beaten

Garnish:

1 jar fruit chutney

Instructions
To prepare, cover a baking sheet with parchment paper, and preheat oven to 400° F.

First make by dough by mixing in a bowl, the Bisquick, cayenne pepper and curry powder. Add warm water and stir until a dough is made. If you need a bit extra water, that's fine. Turn out onto a surfaced that has been sprinkled with some Bisquick and knead 35 times, then set aside.

To make the filling, take a skillet and heat the oil, sauté the garlic, jalapeno and onion until tender. Add allspice, curry and flour, stirring for one minute. Add water and tomato paste then cook another minute until it has thickened. Toss in the chicken and stir. Remove from heat and let cool completely.

Roll the dough on a floured surface to a 14X12 inch rectangle, 1/8 inch in thickness. Cut this into 8 3X6 inch smaller rectangles. Put 1/4 cup filling in the middle of each one, fold in half and seal the edges closed with a fork.

Move these hand pies to the baking sheet and brush with the beaten egg. Bake 20-25 minutes until golden brown. Serve with the chutney. Makes 8 pies.

Spiced Shrimp & Frozen Margarita

1/2 cup lime juice
3 tablespoons tequila
3 tablespoons Triple Sec
1 cup water
1/2 cup sugar
4-1/2 teaspoons grated fine lime peel, divided
1/2 teaspoon salt
1/4 teaspoon ground chipotle pepper
1 teaspoon ground cumin
1 teaspoon smoked paprika
1 teaspoon ground oregano
16 uncooked medium shrimp, peeled and deveined

Instructions
In a pot, cook sugar and water until dissolved. Take off the stove and stir in Triple Sec, 3 t. lime peel, tequila, and lime juice. Cool to room temp, then freeze for 1 hour. Stir with a fork then freeze 4-5 more hours, stirring every half hour until completely frozen.

Mix paprika, oregano, salt, chipotle pepper and cumin in a bowl, then toss in shrimp, stirring to coat. Place shrimp on wooden skewers that have been soaked in water. Lightly oil grill rack, then grill shrimp (or broil in oven), 3 or 4 minutes on each side, until shrimp turns pink.

Just before serving, stir granita with a fork and put into small glasses and top with lime peel for garnish. Serve with the shrimp, makes 8 amazing servings.

County Fair Blue Ribbon Winning Cookbook

Rich Red Wine Sauce with Meatballs

5 ounces milk
6 ounces fresh white bread crumbs
1 teaspoon paprika
5 tablespoons olive oil
1 medium onion, finely chopped
1 pound ground sirloin
1 tablespoon butter
Salt and pepper

Sauce:
1 large clove garlic, minced
8 ounces sliced mushrooms
1 tablespoon butter
4 tablespoons olive oil
2 tablespoons flour
7 ounces beef broth
5 ounces red wine
1 teaspoon brown sugar
1 tablespoon fresh basil, finely chopped
4 tomatoes, peeled and chopped
1 tablespoon tomato paste
Salt and pepper
1-pound package egg noodles, cooked

Instructions
To a bowl add milk and bread crumbs and allow to soak half an hour.

For the sauce, heat oil and 1 T. of butter to a saucepan and add mushrooms and garlic, cooking 4 minutes. Add flour and cook another 2 minutes. Then add wine and broth then simmer 15 minutes. Add basil, brown sugar, tomatoes and tomato paste, salt & pepper, simmer a final half an hour.

Make the meatballs by mixing onions, paprika, bread crumbs milk mixture, and ground sirloin into a bowl with your hands. Form into 14 meatballs and cook in a pan with a small amount of oil, until cooked through the center. Add meatballs to the sauce.

Serve over hot noodles or rice. Another idea is to add to grilled hoagie rolls to make a wonderful meatball sub sandwich. Serves 4-6 people.

Savory Meatball Pie

3/4 cup soft bread crumbs
1/4 cup chopped onion
2 tablespoons minced fresh parsley
1 pound ground beef
1 teaspoon salt
1/2 teaspoon dried marjoram
1/8 teaspoon pepper
1/4 cup milk
1 egg, lightly beaten
1 cup frozen peas
1 cup sliced carrots, cooked
1 can (14-1/2 ounces) stewed tomatoes
1 tablespoon cornstarch
2 teaspoons beef bouillon granules

CRUST:
2-2/3 cups all-purpose flour
1 cup shortening
7 to 8 tablespoons ice water
1/2 teaspoon salt
Half-and-half cream

Instructions
Preheat oven to 400° F.
Mix the first 9 ingredients in a bowl, then divide into fourths. Make 12 small meatballs from each portion. Fry the meatballs in a skillet,

several at a time until cooked through, then drain on paper towels and set aside.

Drain the tomatoes, saving the liquid. Mix this liquid with cornstarch and put into a skillet. Then add bouillon and tomatoes, bringing to a boil on medium heat while constantly stirring. Add carrots and peas, then remove from heat and set aside.

To make the crust, mix salt and flour in a bowl, then cut in shortening until it has the texture of coarse crumbs. Add 1 T. of water at a time, stirring with a fork, until it has a dough texture. Knead gently on a floured surface. When that is complete, divide dough in halves.

Roll each section of dough between 2 sheets of floured wax paper, into a circle that' 1/8 inch in thickness. Remove the waxed paper and move to a 10 inch pie plate. Add meatballs and gently pour the tomato mix on top.

Top the pie with the second half of the rolled dough, trim the edges and flute to seal it. Cut slits in the pie crust and brush with cream.

Bake for 45-50 minutes, covering the edges with foil on the last 15 minutes of baking, so it won't get too dark there. Remove from heat and allow to set for 10 minutes before cutting. Serves 6 people.

Chicken Manicotti Mexican Style

1 package (8 ounces) manicotti shells
1-1/2 cups (6 ounces) shredded cheddar cheese
1 cup (8 ounces) sour cream
2 cups cubed cooked chicken
2 cups (8 ounces) shredded Monterey Jack cheese, divided
1 small onion, diced, divided
1 can (10-3/4 ounces) condensed cream of chicken soup, undiluted
1 cup salsa
2/3 cup milk

Amber Richards

1 can (4 ounces) chopped green chilies, divided

Instructions
While cooking manicotti to directions on the package, add to a bowl, 1 1/2 cups Monterey Jack cheese, cheddar cheese, chicken, sour cream, 6 T. chilies and half the onion.

In a separate bowl, mix the salsa, soup, remaining onion, chilies and milk. Spread 1/2 cup of this to the bottom of a greased 9X13 inch baking dish.

Remove manicotti from heat and rinse in cold water, then drain. Stuff each one with about 1/4 cup of the chicken mix, and place on the sauce on the baking dish. Pour the rest of the sauce over the stuffed manicotti.

Bake at 350° F. covered for 30 minutes. Uncover, then top with the rest of the Monterey Jack cheese and cook 10 more minutes. Makes 7 servings.

Penne Chicken & Gorgonzola Cheese

1 pound boneless skinless chicken breasts, cut into 1/2-inch pieces
1 tablespoon olive oil
1 large garlic clove, minced
1 package (16 ounces) penne pasta
1/4 cup white wine
1 cup heavy whipping cream
1/4 cup chicken broth
6 to 8 fresh sage leaves, thinly sliced
Salt and pepper to taste
2 cups crumbled Gorgonzola cheese
Grated Parmigiano-Reggiano cheese
Minced fresh parsley

County Fair Blue Ribbon Winning Cookbook

Instructions
While cooking pasta to directions on package, brown chicken in oil in a large skillet on medium heat. Add garlic, then add wine and stir to loosen anything that may be wanting to stick to the pan.

Add the broth and cream and cook until it starts to thicken, and the chicken is completely cooked inside. Add to this the sage, salt & pepper and Gorgonzola cheese then simmer until cheese is melted.

Add this sauce with the drained pasta and stir. Top with Parmigiano-Reggiano cheese and parsley. Serves 8 people.

Macaroni & Pepper Jack Cheese

2 cups elbow macaroni (uncooked)
1/2 teaspoon ground mustard
1/2 teaspoon pepper
1/4 cup butter, cubed
1/4 cup all-purpose flour
1/2 teaspoon salt
1/2 teaspoon Worcestershire sauce
1-1/2 cups milk
1/2 cup heavy whipping cream
1 cup shredded sharp cheddar cheese
1/2 cup shredded Asiago cheese
3 cups shredded pepper Jack cheese
1 package (8 ounces) cream cheese, cubed

TOPPING:
1/4 cup grated Parmesan cheese
3/4 cup panko (Japanese) bread crumbs
4 bacon strips, cooked and crumbled
1 cup cheddar French-fried onions, crushed

Instructions
Boil the noodles to directions on package, then drain and set aside.

Melt butter in a large saucepan and stir in flour, mustard, salt & pepper, and Worcestershire sauce. Gently add in cream and milk, then slowly bring to a boil, stirring and cooking for 1 minute until it thickens. Add cheeses and stir until melted. Turn this cheese mixture into the cooked pasta.

Place this in a greased 2 quart baking dish, top with onions, Parmesan cheese, bacon and bread crumbs then bake at 350° F., uncovered for 25 minutes. Makes 6 servings.

Steak Peppered & Port Cherry Sauce Topped

2 beef tenderloin steaks (8 ounces each)
1/2 cup chopped red onion
1/3 cup golden raisins
1/3 cup dried cherries
2 teaspoons coarsely ground pepper
1 cup dry red wine
2 tablespoons sugar
Dash salt
2 teaspoons cold water
1-1/2 teaspoons cornstarch
1/4 teaspoon ground mustard
1/4 cup crumbled blue cheese

Instructions
Pepper the steaks and grill, covered (or broil), on medium heat for 5-8 minutes per side, until it reaches the preferred doneness.

Mix the onion, wine, raisins, sugar and cherries in a small saucepan and bring to a boil. Cook until liquid is reduced by about half.

In a separate bowl, combine water, salt, mustard and cornstarch until smooth. Gradually add this to the saucepan and bring to a boil, stirring for 2 minutes until it thickens. Serve this luscious sauce with the steaks, and top with cheese. Makes 2 servings.

Spinach & Pepperoni Quiche

1 tablespoon olive oil
1 garlic clove, minced
1 tube (8 ounces) refrigerated crescent rolls
1 large sweet red pepper, chopped
5 eggs, lightly beaten
1/2 cup shredded part-skim mozzarella cheese
1/2 cup frozen chopped spinach, thawed and squeezed dry
1/4 cup sliced pepperoni, cut into strips
1/4 cup half-and-half cream
1 tablespoon minced fresh basil or 1 teaspoon dried basil
Dash pepper
2 tablespoons grated Parmesan cheese
1 tablespoon minced fresh parsley

Instructions
Place crescent dough triangles in a 9 inch ungreased fluted pie pan with a removable bottom, with the points facing the center. Press on the bottom and up the sides to make a crust, sealing the seams.

Sauté red pepper with oil until soft in a skillet, then add the garlic, cooking 1 more minute. Remove from heat. In another bowl, mix the rest of the ingredients, then stir in the red pepper. Pour this into the crust you just prepared.

Bake in an oven at 375° F. 30 minutes, until it passes the clean knife test in the center. Remove from heat and allow to set 5 minutes before serving. Makes 8 portions.

Amber Richards

Cornish Hens with Pineapple Stuffing

2 Cornish game hens
1/2 teaspoon salt, divided
1 can (8 ounces) crushed pineapple (save juice)
3 cups cubed day-old bread (1/2-inch cubes), remove crust
2 tablespoons cornstarch
2 tablespoons brown sugar
1 cup cold water
1 tablespoon lemon juice
1 celery rib, chopped
1/2 cup flaked coconut
2/3 cup butter melted, divided
1/4 teaspoon poultry seasoning
2 tablespoons steak sauce

Instructions
Wash, rinse and pat dry the Cornish hens, then sprinkle the insides with a bit of salt, then set aside.

In a bowl, mix the pineapple (reserve the juice), celery, coconut and bread cubes. Add 6 T. of butter then gently stir. Loosely stuff this into the hens, then tie legs together and tuck wings under. Put left over stuffing into a greased baking dish, cover and set aside.

To the remaining butter, add the poultry seasoning, then spoon over the hens. Bake at 350° F. for 40 minutes.

Mix the pineapple juice that was reserved earlier with steak sauce and remaining butter, and baste a couple of times during the baking process.

Uncover the stuffing, then bake both the hens and stuffing for another 30 minutes, or until hens are 185°F and no longer pink inside and 165°F for the stuffing inside the hens.

When done, remove from oven and pour the drippings from the hens into a saucepan. Skim the fat from the surface and add brown sugar, cornstarch, lemon juice and water and mix until smooth. Bring to a gentle boil, stirring constantly for a couple of minutes until thickened. Serve this with the stuffing and hens. Makes 2 servings.

Pizza Waffles

1 egg
2 Tbsp olive oil
2 cups Bisquick
1 1/2 cups whole milk
1 tsp garlic salt
1 tsp Italian seasoning
1/3 cup fresh parmesan cheese, shaved
1 1/4 cup pizza sauce
1 (5 oz) pkg pepperoni
1 (8 oz) pkg fresh mozzarella cheese

Instructions
In a bowl, blend Bisquick, olive oil, egg, garlic salt, milk, parmesan cheese and Italian seasoning together. Pour into a pre-heated waffle iron sprayed with a non-stick cooking spray. When golden brown, remove from heat and allow to cool some, then cut in smaller squares. Spread heated pizza sauce and pepperoni onto half of the waffles, then top with the other half of the waffles, making a sandwich. Put mozzarella cheese on top of this waffle pizza and slightly re-heat in a toaster oven or microwave to melt the cheese. Makes about 5 servings.

Macaroni and Cheese Supreme

2-1/2 cups uncooked elbow macaroni
8 ounces process cheese (Velveeta or American) cut into cubes
1-1/3 cups cottage cheese
6 tablespoons butter, divided
1/4 cup all-purpose flour
1 teaspoon salt

1 teaspoon sugar
2 cups milk
2/3 cup sour cream
2 cups (8 ounces) shredded sharp cheddar cheese
1-1/2 cups soft bread crumbs

Instructions
Cook pasta noodles in boiling water until al dente (not quite soft), then drain. Place noodles in a baking dish sprayed with nonstick cooking spray.

In a pan melt 4 T. of butter, then stir in sugar, salt and flour until smooth. Gradually add milk and bring to a gentle boil. Cook constantly for 2 minutes until thick. Reduce heat, then add American cheese, stirring until that has melted. Add sour cream and cottage cheese.

Pour this mixture over the macaroni and stir gently. Add cheddar cheese to the top.

Melt remaining butter and add to the bread crumbs, then top the macaroni with this.
Bake at 350° F. for 30 minutes, uncovered. Serves 6-8 people.

Roasted Chicken with Lemon Sauce

1 whole chicken for roasting
1/2 teaspoon salt
1/2 teaspoon pepper
6 medium carrots, cut into chunks
1 large onion, quartered
1 medium lemon
1 garlic clove, minced

Lemon Sauce:
2 tablespoons lemon juice

County Fair Blue Ribbon Winning Cookbook

2 tablespoons grated lemon peel
1/2 cup sugar
4-1/2 teaspoons cornstarch
1 cup cold water

Instructions
Wash and rinse chicken, then pat dry. Take half a lemon and squeeze the juice on the chicken, then place the lemon in the cavity. Sprinkle salt & pepper on chicken and rub garlic on the skin of the chicken. Place chicken in a preheated oven at 350° F. in a roasting pan and cook about 2 - 2 1/2 hours or until temp reaches 173°F at the thickest part.

Add onions and carrots to the pan during the last hour, and baste occasionally with the pan juices. You may want to cover the chicken with aluminum foil the last hour as well, if it is browning too fast. When done, remove from heat and allow to sit 15 minutes before cutting, this helps it to remain moist.

In a small pan mix the cornstarch and sugar together, then add the water and bring to a slow boil until thickened. Remove from heat and add lemon peel and juice. Serve the chicken with this sauce (it would be good over steamed vegetables too).

Dumplings & Round Steak

3/4 cup flour
1 medium onion, chopped
2-2/3 cups water
1 tablespoon paprika
3 pounds boneless beef top round steak, cut into serving-size pieces
2 tablespoons canola oil
2 cans (10-3/4 ounces each) condensed cream of chicken soup, undiluted
1/2 teaspoon pepper

DUMPLINGS:
3 cups flour
1-1/2 teaspoons celery salt
1-1/2 teaspoons poultry seasoning
1/4 cup dried minced onion 2 tablespoons baking powder
1 tablespoon poppy seeds
3/4 teaspoon salt
1 cup dry bread crumbs
1/4 cup butter, melted
1-1/2 cups milk
6 tablespoons canola oil

Instructions
Mix flour and paprika in a large plastic bag that can be resealed. Add a few pieces of beef at a time, and shake to coat.

Put oil in a medium high heat pan and cook the beef, then set the beef aside. Sauté onion in the drippings until it becomes soft. Add water, soup and pepper then cook until it boils. Place this mixture and the beef, in a large baking pan with a lid. Cover and bake at 325° for 1 hour.

For dumplings, mix the flour, minced onion, celery salt, baking powder, poppy seeds, poultry seasoning and salt in a bowl. Add milk and oil in a bowl, then stir in dry ingredients. Leave it for about 3 minutes, until it moistens.

Increase the heat to a temperature of 425° F. Mix breadcrumbs and butter in a large bowl. Take a tablespoon with the dumplings mix, and roll it into the crumb mixture. Now place this on top of simmering beef mixture.

Cover and bake about 20-25 minutes longer until a toothpick inserted in a dumpling comes out clean. Don't remove the lid on the baking dish while cooking the dumplings until they are done. Makes 10-12 servings

Seafood Lasagna

8 ounces clam juice
1 green onion, finely chopped
1 pound bay scallops
1 pound uncooked small shrimp, peeled and deveined
1 can (8 ounces) crabmeat
2 tablespoons canola oil
2 tablespoons plus 1/2 cup butter, divided
1/2 cup chicken broth
1 cup heavy whipping cream
1/2 cup shredded Parmesan cheese, divided
9 lasagna noodles, cooked and drained
1/4 teaspoon white pepper, divided
1/2 cup flour
1-1/2 cups milk
1/2 teaspoon salt

Instructions
Sauce onion in oil and 2 T. of butter in a skillet until tender. Add clam juice and broth then allow to boil. Add crab, shrimp, scallops and

pepper, reduce heat and simmer about 5 minutes, until shrimp is pink & scallops are opaque and firm. Drain and reserve the liquid. Put the seafood in a different container.

Melt the remaining butter in a saucepan, add flour and stir until smooth. Gradually stir in the reserved cooking liquid from above and milk, salt and pepper and cook until it boils, stirring constantly. Allow it to thicken about 2 minutes, then add cream and 1/4 cup cheese. Now mix 3/4 cup of this sauce into the cooked seafood that was set aside.

In a greased 9x13 baking dish, spread 1/2 cup of the white sauce on the bottom. Place 3 noodles on top, then layer half of the seafood, 1 1/4 cups of the white sauce, and repeat. Top the last layer with all remaining sauce and cheese.

Bake at 350° F. uncovered for 40 minutes. Remove from heat and allow to set 15 minutes before cutting. Makes 12 servings.

Caribbean Pot Roast Slow Cooked

1 boneless beef chuck roast (2-1/2 pounds)
2 medium sweet potatoes, cubed
2 large carrots, sliced
1/4 cup chopped celery
1 tablespoon canola oil
1 large onion, chopped
2 garlic cloves, minced
1 tablespoon all-purpose flour
1 tablespoon sugar
1 tablespoon brown sugar
3/4 teaspoon grated orange peel
3/4 teaspoon baking cocoa
1 can (15 ounces) tomato sauce
1 teaspoon ground cumin
3/4 teaspoon salt
3/4 teaspoon ground coriander
3/4 teaspoon chili powder

County Fair Blue Ribbon Winning Cookbook

1/2 teaspoon dried oregano
1/8 teaspoon ground cinnamon

Instructions
Place carrots, celery and potatoes, in a slow cooker. In a skillet, brown meat in oil on all sides, then add garlic & onion, cook until tender. Add sugar, brown sugar, flour, seasonings, orange peel and cocoa. Gently stir in tomato sauce. Transfer this to the slow cooker.

Cook on low heat for 6 to 8 hours or until beef and vegetables are tender. Serves 10.

Tamale Pie Slow Cooked

1 pound hamburger
1 can (15 ounces) black beans, rinsed and drained
1 can (14-1/2 ounces) diced tomatoes with mild green chilies, undrained
1 can (11 ounces) whole kernel corn, drained
1 teaspoon ground cumin
1/2 teaspoon salt
1/2 teaspoon chili powder
1/4 teaspoon pepper
1 can (10 ounces) enchilada sauce
1 package (8-1/2 ounces) corn bread/muffin mix
2 eggs
1 cup (4 ounces) shredded Mexican cheese blend
2 green onions, chopped
1/4 cup minced fresh cilantro
Sour cream and additional minced fresh cilantro, optional

Instructions
In a large skillet, cook beef over medium heat until fully cooked. Drain and then stir in the cumin, salt, chili powder and pepper.

Move to a slow cooker; add the corn, enchilada sauce, beans, tomatoes, onions and cilantro. Cover and cook on low 6-8 hours.

Add the corn bread mix and eggs in a small bowl and mix. Add meat mixture to the slow cooker. Cover and cook for about 1 hour or until a knife inserted near the center comes out clean.

Sprinkle cheese over the mixture and cover. Allow to set for 5 minutes. Serve with sour cream. Makes 8 servings.

Adobo-Lime Southwest Hash

1 tablespoon canola oil
1 teaspoon garlic powder
1 teaspoon smoked paprika
3 medium sweet potatoes (about 1-1/2 pounds), cubed
1 medium onion, chopped
1 medium sweet red pepper, chopped
3/4 teaspoon ground chipotle pepper
1/2 teaspoon salt
1/4 teaspoon pepper
2/3 cup canned black beans, rinsed and drained
2 teaspoons adobo sauce
1/2 medium ripe avocado, peeled and sliced, optional
2 tablespoons minced fresh cilantro
4 eggs
1/2 cup reduced-fat sour cream
2 tablespoons lime juice

Instructions
Preheat oven to 400°. Place onion and red pepper and sweet potatoes, in a 10X15 baking pan sprayed with cooking spray. Drizzle with oil; sprinkle seasonings on top, then stir. Roast in the oven for 25-30 minutes until potatoes are soft. Add beans during the last 10 minutes.

County Fair Blue Ribbon Winning Cookbook

Place 2-3 in. of water in a large saucepan and bring to a boil, then reduce heat to maintain a gentle simmer. Break cold eggs, one at a time, into a small bowl. Gently slip the eggs into the saucepan of water.

Cook uncovered for 3-5 minutes until whites are completely set and yolks thicken but are not hard. Carefully lift the eggs out of water with a slotted spoon and place on top of roasted sweet potatoes.

Mix lime juice, adobo sauce and sour cream, in a small bowl.

Serve sweet potatoes with the egg and sour cream topping.

Sprinkle with cilantro. You can also serve with avocado if you wish. Makes 4 servings.

Sausage Bake Southwest Style

10 eggs, lightly beaten
1/2 cup milk
1/2 teaspoon each salt, garlic salt, onion salt, pepper and ground cumin
Paprika
6 flour tortillas (10 inches), cut into 1/2-inch strips
4 cans (4 ounces each) chopped green chilies, drained
1 pound premium pork sausage cooked and drained
2 cups (8 ounces) shredded Monterey Jack cheese
2 medium tomatoes, sliced
Sour cream and salsa

Instructions
Grease a 9X13 baking dish and layer half the tortilla strips, sausage, chilies, cheese, then repeat the layers.

Whisk the milk, seasonings and eggs in a bowl, then pour over the above ingredients in the baking dish. Top with cheese, cover and chill overnight.

Amber Richards

Bake uncovered at 350° for 50 minutes. Remove from heat, then arrange tomato slices over the top. Bake it for 10-15 minutes longer. Remove from heat and allow to sit 10 minutes before cutting. Serve with salsa and sour cream. Makes 12 servings.

Cheesy Spiced Chicken Bowl

3/4 cup milk
1 1/3 lbs skinless chicken breasts
2 3/4 cups Bisquick
3/4 cup sharp cheddar cheese, finely shredded
Salt
Pepper
1/2 cup sweet chili sauce
1 cup chicken broth
1 cup radishes, sliced
1/4 cup snow peas, cut into pieces
1 cup romaine lettuce, chopped
1 cup green leaf lettuce, chopped
1/4 cup carrots, julienned
8 thinly sliced onion rings
2 mini peppers, seeded and cut into rings

Instructions
Mix cheese and Bisquick in a bowl, then add milk. Knead gently 10 times, then divide into 4 pieces. Roll each piece on a lightly floured surface to 1/8 inch thick. Put in 5 inch aluminum pie tins, press and flute the edges for little mini pies. Bake at 425°F for 8 minutes, then cool completely.

Add salt & pepper to chicken and place in a saucepan over medium heat. Add broth and chili sauce, and bring to a boil. Cook chicken until it is no longer pink, about 10 minutes, turning once during the cooking.

Allow pan to cool and remove the chicken. Strain the liquid and reserve it.

Mix radishes, snow peas, lettuce and carrots together. Divide equally into each bread bowl, then add to each one 3 pepper rings and 2 onion rings. Slice chicken and add to the top. Finally pour broth over chicken, then serve. Makes 4 servings.

Pork with Maple Ginger Sauce

1/2 tsp. salt
2 tsp. chili powder
1 tsp. ground cinnamon
1 tsp. pepper
1/4 tsp. ground allspice
1 pork tenderloin (3/4 pound)
1/2 tsp. olive oil

SAUCE:
1 tsp. chopped gingerroot
1/2 c. chicken broth
1/2 c. chopped onion
1 tablespoon butter
1/4 c. maple syrup
1 T. chopped crystallized ginger

Instructions
Add cinnamon, pepper, chili powder, salt and allspice in a small bowl. Rub on pork, then brown the pork in a large skillet in oil on both all sides.

Put in a 7x11 baking dish sprayed with cooking spray. Bake at 375° F, uncovered until pork is thoroughly cooked inside.

While this is cooking, sauté onion in butter until tender, add ginger and sauté another 2 minutes. Add the syrup, candied ginger and broth and allow it to boil. Cook until sauce has reduced in volume to about 1/2 cup.

Pour this over the pork and bake 5-10 minutes longer.

Crab Spinach Chicken

3 tablespoons butter
3 tablespoons flour
1/2 cup finely chopped onion
1/4 cup chopped fresh mushrooms
1/4 cup chopped celery
1/2 teaspoon salt, divided
1/2 cup dry bread crumbs
1 can (6 ounces) crabmeat, drained
12 fresh chopped spinach leaves
1 tablespoon cut fresh parsley
1 cup chicken broth
1/2 cup milk
4 boneless skinless chicken breasts (6 ounces each)
1/8 teaspoon white pepper
1 cup shredded Swiss cheese
Cooked rice, hot (enough for 4 servings)

Instructions
To make the sauce, sauté mushrooms, celery and onion in butter in a skillet until tender. Stir in 1/4 tsp. salt and flour. Gradually add milk and broth, then bring to a boil, stirring 2 minutes until thick. Remove from heat.

Flatten chicken to 1/4 inch thick, sprinkle with salt & pepper. In a bowl, mix the crab, parsley, spinach and bread crumbs; stir in 1/2 cup of the sauce. Take 1/4 cup of this mixture onto the center of each chicken breast half, then roll and secure with a toothpick.

Place the chicken, seam side down, in a greased 9x13 baking dish, then pour the rest of the sauce over. Cover and bake in a 375° F. oven 45 minutes, until chicken is fully cooked. Sprinkle with cheese, then broil 5 minutes until lightly browned. Serve with rice, makes 4 servings.

Pulled Beef Sweet and Savory Dinner

Ingredients
1 teaspoon paprika
1 teaspoon chili powder
1 teaspoon salt
1 teaspoon ground mustard
1 teaspoon barbecue seasoning
1/2 teaspoon pepper
1 large onion, halved and sliced
1 large sweet red pepper, sliced
1 boneless beef chuck roast (3 pounds)
3 tablespoons olive oil

SAUCE:
2 tablespoons Dijon mustard
2 tablespoons Worcestershire sauce
1 can (8 ounces) tomato sauce
1/3 cup packed brown sugar
3 tablespoons honey
4 teaspoons balsamic vinegar
3/4 teaspoon salt
2 tablespoons soy sauce
5 garlic cloves, minced
Cooked egg noodles

Instructions

Mix the first six ingredients. Cut roast in half and rub with seasonings. In a large skillet, roll the beef in oil and let it brown on all sides. Move to a slow cooker. Add the red pepper and onion.

Add the mustard, Worcestershire sauce, tomato sauce, brown sugar, honey, soy sauce, salt, garlic, and vinegar in a small bowl. Place the vegetables over the beef, then pour the sauce over. Cook, covered on low heat for 6-8 hours.

Remove the roast and allow it to cool some. Shred beef with two forks and then move it back to the crockpot to simmer and re-heat. Serve over cooked noodles. Makes 6 servings.

Beef Brisket with a Tangy Twist

1-1/2 cups packed brown sugar
1/2 cup Worcestershire sauce
1 large onion, diced
1/2 cup butter
1 bottle (28 ounces) ketchup
1/3 cup lemon juice
2 tablespoons chili powder
1 teaspoon prepared horseradish
1/2 teaspoon garlic powder
1-1/2 teaspoons hot pepper sauce
1 teaspoon salt
1 boneless beef brisket (about 6 pounds)

Instructions
Sauté onion in butter until soft. Add the next nine ingredients then allow it to boil. Reduce the heat and cook on low, uncovered for 35 minutes.

Put beef brisket in roasting pan and add 3 cups of the sauce. Cover and bake at 350° F. for 4 hours or until tender. Basting occasionally during the cooking time. When done, remove from pan and thinly slice across the grain. Top with remaining sauce. Makes 12-14 servings.

Onion & Turkey Bacon Spirals

Dough:
1 teaspoon sugar
1 package dry yeast
2 large eggs, beaten
2/3 cup lukewarm milk (110 degrees)
3 cups all-purpose flour
1 teaspoon salt
2/3 cup butter, diced and softened

Filling:
2 cups onion, finely chopped
2 garlic cloves, finely sliced
8 ounces turkey bacon, cut into small pieces
1 tablespoon butter
1 teaspoon fresh thyme, finely chopped
1 large egg yolk
2 tablespoons milk

Instructions
Place sugar and yeast in a bowl with the scalded milk. Let it set 10 minutes until it begins to foam. Add the flour and salt in a large mixer bowl with dough hooks on the mixer attachment. Add the mixture of yeast and eggs and begin mixing. Gradually add butter until the dough becomes elastic and is smooth in texture. This should take about 5 minutes. Roll it into a ball and place in a greased bowl, cover with a clean cloth. Set aside for 1 hour or until doubled in size.

For the filling while dough is rising, cook bacon in a frying pan until crisp. Add the onion, butter, and garlic. Simmer on low 10 minutes until it becomes tender. Add the thyme, remove from heat and allow to cool.

Rub your hands with flour, then punch down the risen dough, and knead on a floured surface. Roll this into 2 12x8-inch rectangles about 1/4-

inch thick. Spread cooled filling on the dough evenly. Start from the short side, roll each rectangle into a log shape. Cut into 3/4-inch slices.

Add parchment paper to a baking sheet and place the cut slices 2-inches apart. Cover and allow it to rise again, in a warm place for 20 to 30 minutes. Preheat the oven to 375° F.

Whisk egg yolk with the milk, then brush the spirals. Bake for a period of 15 to 20 minutes or until it turns light brown. Then transfer it to cooling rack. Serve while warm or at room temperature. Makes 12 - 15 servings.

Primavera A La Turkey

Ingredients
3 tablespoons butter
4 large fresh mushrooms, sliced
1/2 cup chopped yellow summer squash
1/2 cup chopped zucchini
1 cup uncooked penne pasta
8 fresh asparagus spears, trimmed and cut into 1-inch pieces
2/3 cup julienned carrot
1-1/2 cups shredded cooked turkey
1 envelope Italian salad dressing mix
1 cup heavy whipping cream
1 medium tomato, chopped
1/4 cup grated Parmesan cheese

Instructions
In a large skillet, sauté carrot and asparagus in butter for 3 minutes. Add the yellow squash, mushrooms, and zucchini then sauté until it is tender, yet still a bit crisp. Cook pasta according to package directions.

Stir in the tomato, dressing mix, turkey, and cream. Allow it to boil. Cook while stirring for 2 minutes.

Drain the pasta. Pour it in the vegetable mixture, top with cheese and toss it to mix. Makes 4 servings.

Chicken Piccata

1 teaspoon chicken bouillon, ground fine with small coffee grinder, or substitute 1 teaspoon salt
2 teaspoons pepper
1 1/4 cup flour
½ teaspoon poultry seasoning
½ teaspoon Lawry's seasoned salt
¼ cup olive or canola oil, divided
1 pound sliced mushrooms
2 ¾ cups white wine
3 ½ ounces capers, drained
¼ cup salted butter
2 ½ pounds chicken tenders
2 small lemons, sliced
Parsley (optional)

Instructions
Mix all seasonings and flour. Place this mixture in a plastic bag. Add 2 T. of olive oil to a large skillet. Sauté mushrooms partially. Remove from heat and strain.

Put a couple chicken tenders in flour mixture and shake to coat. Combine the butter and remaining oil in the fry pan and brown the chicken.

Add wine and mushrooms to the chicken. Bring to a boil, then reduce heat. Simmer for 15 minutes until chicken is completely cooked, and wine has been reduced. Feel free to use additional wine if it evaporates too quickly, and moisture is lacking.

Put sliced lemons on top of chicken tenders, then top with capers. Garnish with parsley.
Serves 6.

Ultimate Lasagna

1/2 cup Burgundy wine
2 tablespoons brown sugar
2 jars (24 ounces each) meatless spaghetti sauce
1 can (14-1/2 ounces) diced tomatoes, drained
3 garlic cloves, minced
2 pounds Italian turkey sausage links, casings removed
3/4 cup raisins
2 eggs, lightly beaten
2 cartons 15 ounces each ricotta cheese
2 teaspoons Italian seasoning
1-1/2 pounds sliced fresh mushrooms
1 medium onion, chopped
1 package (10 ounces) frozen chopped spinach, thawed and squeezed dry
1 cup grated Parmesan cheese
2 packages (24 ounces each) frozen cheese ravioli, thawed
6 cups (24 ounces) shredded Monterey Jack cheese
5 large tomatoes, sliced
1 cup shredded Parmesan cheese
18 slices provolone cheese, cut in half

Instructions
In a Dutch oven, bring first five ingredients to a boil. Reduce heat; simmer, uncovered, for 20 minutes or until desired thickness is achieved, stirring often.

Boil the first five ingredients in a Dutch oven. Reduce the heat. Simmer uncovered for 20 minutes, stir often.

Cook sausage over medium heat in a large skillet until fully cooked through, then drain. Stir in Italian seasoning and raisins and add to the sauce. Sauté onion and mushrooms until all the moisture has evaporated, then add this to the sauce. Mix the ricotta cheese, eggs, spinach and grated Parmesan cheese in a large bowl, then set aside.

Grease 2 9X13 baking dishes then layer the following in each of them. 1 1/3 cup of the sauce, half the ravioli, another 1 1/3 cup of sauce, 1/4 cup Parmesan cheese, 1/2 of the provolone cheese, tomatoes, then Monterey Jack cheese. Now layer the second half of the ravioli, and 2 1/2 cups of the spinach mixture.

Finish topping these with the remaining provolone cheese, remaining sauce and ravioli, Monterey Jack cheese and Parmesan cheese, then sliced tomatoes.

Bake covered in a 375° F oven for 45 minutes. Remove the cover then cook another 15 minutes. Remove from heat and allow to set for 15 minutes before cutting. Makes 2 casseroles 12 servings each.

Vegetables & Salads

Coleslaw with Blueberries

½ cup thinly sliced onion
1 carrot, julienned
1 head Savoy cabbage, thinly shredded
3 cups blueberries
1 cup mayonnaise
1 tablespoon cumin seeds, toasted
1 teaspoon salt
2 tablespoons red wine vinegar
1 tablespoon honey

Instructions

Cut the cabbage into thin shreds and mix in a large bowl with the carrot, blueberries and onion. In another bowl combine the mayo, honey, vinegar, salt and cumin seeds. Pour over the cabbage mixture and toss, then chill. Makes 8 Servings

Bread & Butter Banana Peppers

1 small onion, sliced
2-1/2 c. seeded & cut banana peppers (7 peppers)
1 green pepper, julienned or 1 medium green tomato sliced
1 seeded and sliced jalapeno pepper
1/4 c. canning salt
15 ice cubes
1 T. mustard seed
1/2 tsp celery seed
2 c. sugar
1 c. white vinegar

Amber Richards

Instructions
Mix onion, peppers and salt in a big bowl, then top with ice. Allow this to set for 2 hours, then rinse and drain.

Mix vinegar, mustard seed, celery seed and sugar in a pan, then bring to a boil, stirring until sugar is dissolved. Pour this over the peppers, then chill at least 24 hours before serving. Store in an air tight container, makes 1 quart.

Grilled Chicken with Brown Rice Salad

2/3 c. chopped green onions
1/2 c. pecans, chopped
3 T. minced parsley
3 c. cooked brown rice
2 c. chicken breasts cooked and cut
2 chopped apples
1 chopped sweet red pepper
2 chopped celery ribs
1 T. lemon juice
1 tsp salt
1/4 tsp. pepper
1/4 c. cider vinegar
3 T. canola oil

Instructions
Mix the first 8 ingredients into a large bowl. In a separate bowl whisk the oil, salt & pepper, lemon juice and vinegar, then pour over the salad and toss. Ready to serve. Makes 9 servings.

County Fair Blue Ribbon Winning Cookbook

Superb Corn Salad

1 c. chopped green onions
1/2 c. shredded Parmesan cheese
2 tsp. ground cumin
2 packages (10 ounces each) frozen corn, thawed
2 c. chopped green pepper
2 c. chopped sweet red pepper
2 c. chopped celery
1 cup minced fresh parsley
1-1/2 tsp. salt
3/4 tsp. pepper
1/2 tsp. hot pepper sauce
1/8 tsp. cayenne pepper
2 garlic minced cloves
6 T. lime juice
3 T. olive oil

Instructions
Mix the first twelve ingredients in a large bowl. In a separate bowl mix the garlic and oil, then microwave for 30 seconds on high. Allow to cool, then stir in lime juice. Pour over the salad and toss. Cover and chill before serving. Makes 16-18 servings.

Mandarin Broccoli Salad

CUSTARD DRESSING:
1 teaspoon ground mustard
1/4 cup white vinegar
1/4 cup water
1/2 cups sugar
1-1/2 teaspoons cornstarch
1 egg plus 1 egg yolk, lightly beaten
3 tablespoons butter, softened
1/2 cup mayonnaise

SALAD:
1 can (11 ounces) mandarin oranges, drained
6 slices bacon, cooked and crumbled
1/2 cup slivered almonds, toasted
1/2 cup golden raisins
4 cups fresh broccoli florets, 1-inch cuts
2 cups sliced fresh mushrooms
1/2 medium red onion, sliced in 1/8-inch-thick rings

Instructions
Mix cornstarch, sugar, and mustard in a large saucepan. Add water and vinegar then blend until smooth. Cook while stirring over medium-high heat until it is bubbly and thick. Lower the heat, then cook for another 2 minutes, then remove from the heat source.

Blend a little bit of this hot filling into an egg and yolk, stir well. Pour this back into the pan and while stirring constantly, bring to a boil, cooking it for 2 minutes. Remove from heat and stir in butter and mayonnaise then allow to cool to room temperature, not stirring anymore. Chill once it has reached room temp.

Put the onion, oranges, bacon, broccoli, mushrooms, almonds and raisins in a large salad bowl. Drizzle the dressing over the salad and toss. It's now ready to enjoy, makes 10-12 servings.

Vegetable Lasagna

2 julienned large carrots
2 julienned sweet red peppers
1/4 c. olive oil
2 zucchini, cut diagonally
2 c. broccoli florets
2 minced garlic cloves
1/2 tsp. salt
1/2 tsp. pepper
3/4 tsp. dried thyme

SAUCE:
2 cans (28 ounces each) crushed tomatoes
3 tsp. Italian seasoning
3/4 tsp. salt
3/4 tsp. pepper
2 c. chopped Portobello mushrooms
1 chopped onion
2 minced garlic cloves
2 T. olive oil

FILLING:
3/4 c. grated Parmesan cheese
1 egg, lightly beaten
2 tsp. dried basil
1-1/4 c. ricotta cheese
1 package (8 ounces) cream cheese, softened

ASSEMBLY:
3 c. shredded Italian cheese blend
12 no-cook lasagna noodles

Instructions

Before beginning, you'll want to preheat your oven to 425°F. In a large bowl, put the first 9 ingredients inside, then toss gently. Take 2 greased 10X15 baking pans and place the mixture inside. Bake for 10-15 minutes, stirring a couple of times, until tender. Reduce oven heat to 350° F.

In a saucepan, sauté garlic, onions and mushrooms in oil until soft. Add the remaining sauce ingredients and bring to a gentle boil. Reduce heat and allow to simmer 10 minutes or so.

In another bowl, mix the filling ingredients. Use a greased 9X13 baking dish and layer the following: 1 cup sauce, 1/3 of the noodles, 1/3 of the ricotta cheese blend, half of the vegetables, 1/3 of the remaining sauce, 1/3 of the cheese blend, then repeat. Finish with remaining noodles, sauce, ricotta mix, and cheese. Cover and cook 40 minutes. Remove from heat and allow to set for 15 minutes before cutting. Makes 12 servings.

Fresh Cucumber & Tomato Salad

1 teaspoon minced fresh mint or 1/4 teaspoon dried mint
1/8 teaspoon kosher salt
1/8 teaspoon coarsely ground pepper
1/4 cup lemon juice
1/4 cup olive oil
1 tablespoon minced fresh basil or 1 teaspoon dried basil
1 tablespoon white wine vinegar
1 garlic clove, minced
1/2 cup Greek olives, sliced
2 cups torn mixed salad greens
4 plum tomatoes, seeded and chopped
2 medium cucumbers, chopped
1/4 cup pine nuts, toasted
3/4 cup crumbled feta cheese

County Fair Blue Ribbon Winning Cookbook

Instructions
Whisk the first 8 ingredients together in bowl, then set aside. Combine cucumbers, olives and tomatoes into a large bowl. Pour in half the dressing and toss lightly. Place salad greens on a plate and spoon cucumber mixture on top. Sprinkle with pine nuts and cheese, then drizzle last part of dressing on top. Makes 6 servings.

Bacon, Green Pea And Cashew Salad

3 T. mayonnaise
2 T. dry ranch dressing mix
1 c. sour cream
1 c. cashew halves
10 ounces peas
¼ c. chopped red onion
¼ c. chopped red bell pepper
¾ c. sliced water chestnuts
½ lb. bacon, fried crisp and crumbled
½ c. chopped celery

Instructions
Mix the dressing by combining dressing mix, mayonnaise and sour cream.

Add bacon, celery, onion, water chestnuts, pepper and peas in a large bowl. Add dressing, stir well and chill. Right before serving, mix in cashews. Makes 6 to 8 servings.

Amber Richards

Mushroom & Green Bean Pie

3 cups sliced fresh mushrooms
2-1/2 cups chopped onions
6 cups cut fresh green beans (1-inch pieces)
4 tablespoons butter, divided
2 teaspoons minced fresh thyme or 3/4 teaspoon dried thyme
1 package (8 ounces) cream cheese, cubed
1/2 cup milk
1/2 teaspoon salt
1/4 teaspoon pepper

CRUST:
2-1/2 cups all-purpose flour
1/4 teaspoon salt
1 cup cold butter, cubed
2 teaspoons baking powder
1 teaspoon dill weed
1 cup (8 ounces) sour cream
1 egg
1 tablespoon heavy whipping cream

Instructions
Sauté the mushrooms in 1 T. of butter in a large skillet, until soft, drain then set aside. Sauté beans and onions in the same skillet with the rest of the butter for 10 minutes, until beans are tender, but slightly crisp. Add salt, pepper, thyme, milk, cream cheese and mushrooms, then cook until cheese is melted and smooth. Remove from heat.

Mix the flour, salt, dill and baking powder in a bowl. Cut in the butter with a pastry knife until it has the texture of coarse crumbs. Add sour cream and stir for a soft dough, then divide it in half. Roll half on a well floured surface to fit a deep dish 9 inch pie pan, then trim the edge. Roll the other half of the dough to make a lattice crust top.

Pour the bean blend into the pie crust, top with the lattice top, then flute the edges to seal. Beat the egg and cream in a small bowl and brush over the lattice top. Bake in a 400° F. oven for 30 minutes. Makes 8-10 servings.

Veggie Sandwich Grilled

1 sweet red pepper, sliced
1 small red onion, cut up
1 zucchini, sliced thin lengthwise
1/4 c. Italian salad dressing
1 loaf ciabatta bread
2 T. olive oil
2 tsp lemon zest
1 tsp. garlic, minced
1/4 c. mayonnaise
1 T. lemon juice
1/2 c. crumbled feta cheese

Instructions
Place the onion, pepper, zucchini and salad dressing in a re-sealable plastic bag, gently shake and chill at least 1 hour. Drain and toss out the dressing.

Cut bread and brush the inside with oil, then set aside. Put veggies on a grill rack and grill covered on medium heat 4-5 minutes on each side. Remove from heat, yet keep warm. Grill bread, oil side down until toasted.

Mix the lemon juice, mayonnaise, lemon peel and garlic in a small bowl. Spread over bread, the sprinkle with cheese. Place vegetables and bread top on, then cut into 4 servings. Yum!

Amber Richards

Mediterranean Vegetables Grilled

1 medium zucchini, sliced
10 fresh asparagus spears, cut into 2-inch lengths
1 small onion, sliced and separated into rings
3/4 cup grape tomatoes
3 large Portobello mushrooms, sliced
1 each medium sweet red, orange and yellow peppers. sliced
1/2 cup fresh sugar snap peas
1/2 cup fresh broccoli florets
1/2 cup pitted Greek olives
1 bottle (14 ounces) Greek vinaigrette
1/2 cup feta cheese, crumbed

Instructions
Combine all the vegetables in a re-sealable plastic bag, with the vinaigrette. Seal the bag and gently toss to coat all the vegetables, then chill for a minimum of 30 minutes.

Drain the vegetables, then move to a grill and cook on medium heat for 8-12 minutes until tender, stirring while cooking. Sprinkle with cheese and serve. Makes 9 servings.

Mediterranean Pasta & Vegetables

3 ounces uncooked angel hair pasta
1/3 cup chopped green pepper
1 cup chopped zucchini
1/2 cup chopped fresh mushrooms
1/4 cup chopped onion
2 teaspoons olive oil
1 garlic clove, minced
1/8 teaspoon pepper
1 cup canned Italian diced tomatoes
6 pitted ripe olives, halved
1/4 cup crumbled feta cheese

1 tablespoon shredded Parmesan cheese

Instructions
According to package directions, cook pasta. While this is cooking, in a skillet, sauté green pepper, onion, mushrooms, and zucchini in oil until they are tender, yet crisp. Add garlic and cook 1 more minute. Add olives, tomatoes and pepper then heat through.

Drain pasta and place on a serving plate. Top with the vegetables and cheese. Makes 2 servings.

Cheesy Carrots

2 teaspoons chicken bouillon granules
2 pounds carrots, sliced
1 package (8 ounces) cream cheese, cubed
8 ounces process cheese (Velveeta or American), cubed
2 tablespoons butter
4 green onions, sliced
1/4 teaspoon salt
1/4 teaspoon pepper

Instructions
In a large saucepan add 1 inch of water to the bottom, then bouillon and carrots then bring to a boil. Reduce heat then simmer (covered) for 8 minutes until carrots are tender, yet crisp.

In another saucepan, melt butter and cheese on low heat. When that has melted, add onions, cream cheese, salt and pepper and cook until cream cheese is liquid.

Take a greased baking dish and add drained carrots and cheese sauce. Bake at 350° F. covered for 25 minutes. Makes 8 servings.

Zucchini Fries

3/4 cup fresh grated Parmesan cheese
1 cup Bisquick mix
1 1/2 tablespoons garlic herb seasoning
1 tablespoon water
1 egg
2-3 small zucchini, washed and cut strips

Instructions
Combine garlic seasoning, bisquick and cheese in a bowl. In another bowl whisk the water and egg together. Dip the zucchini in the egg wash, and then coat with the bisquick mix. Put on a greased cookie sheet, then bake at 425°F. for 20 - 25 minutes until golden brown. You might want to turn the fries over halfway through the baking time.

Serve with either marinara sauce or ranch dressing.

Sweet Potatoes Delight

1/2 C. pitted prunes, presoaked, cut into quarters
1 T. grated orange rind
2 lbs. sweet potatoes cooked and quartered
1, 20-oz. can crushed pineapple, undrained
1 T. butter
1/2 C. slivered almonds

Instructions
Mix the first 4 ingredients in a bowl, then pour into a greased 1 quart casserole dish. Top with almonds and butter. Bake at 350°F for 45 minutes. Serves 6-8 people.

Spinach Salad

2 tablespoons plus 2 teaspoons red wine vinegar
2 tablespoons plus 2 teaspoons sugar
1/2 cup canola oil
1/4 cup chopped onion
1-1/2 teaspoons ground mustard
1/2 teaspoon salt
1-1/2 teaspoons poppy seeds
8 cups torn fresh organic spinach
3 large ripe bananas, cut into 1/2-inch slices
3 green onions, sliced
2 pints fresh strawberries, sliced
1/2 cup slivered almonds, toasted

Instructions
Whip the first 6 ingredients in a blender, until sugar is dissolved. Add poppy seeds and give it one final quick blend, just to get them mixed in.

Combine the salad ingredients into a large salad bowl, then add the dressing and toss. Makes 14 servings.

Cranberry & Sweet Potato Crepes

Crepes
½ teaspoon cinnamon
½ teaspoon nutmeg
½ teaspoon salt
1 ½ cup flour
1 ¼ cup baked sweet potato, cooled and peeled
2½-3 cup milk
2 Tablespoon butter, melted
1 Tablespoon brown sugar
1 teaspoon vanilla
2 eggs at room temperature

Filling:
¾ teaspoon cinnamon
¾ teaspoon nutmeg
1 teaspoon orange zest
2 cup heavy cream, chilled
¾ cup brown sugar
1 teaspoon vanilla

Cranberry Sauce:
1 whole cranberry sauce (14 oz. can)
¼ cup orange marmalade

Toppings & Garnish:
Honey or Maple Syrup
Remaining canned whole cranberries
¾ cup chopped toasted pecans
3 Tablespoons granulated sugar
Confectioners' sugar

Instructions

To make the crepes mix brown sugar, flour, salt, cinnamon and nutmeg in a bowl together. In a separate bowl, mix with a hand mixer the sweet potatoes until smooth. Gradually add the milk, then vanilla and butter and mix well. Add in the dry ingredients you just mixed, in small portions, beating slowly. When completed the batter will be thin. If it has the texture of pancake batter, add a bit more milk so it is thinner. Chill for a minimum of half an hour.

Heat a skillet sprayed with cooking spray on medium high heat. Pour 1/4 cup of batter
in the middle of the pan, instantly pick up the pan and gently swirl the batter in a circle so it spreads out to a 6 inch circle. Cook until the edge starts to get light brown and the middle is no longer liquid, then gently flip the crepe over. Cook 15-30 seconds on the second side. Remove and set on a plate to cool.

For the filling, put the whipping cream in a chilled metal bowl and beat with a mixer until stiff. Add zest, vanilla and brown sugar cinnamon, nutmeg, until just mixed. Chill in refrigerator until you are ready to assemble the crepes.

To make the cranberry portion, in a small bowl mix the marmalade and 1 cup of whole cranberry sauce (reserve the remaining).

For the garnish and toppings, toast the pecans by putting them in a small pan on medium heat for 5 minutes, stirring a couple of times. Then take out a few whole cranberries from the remaining cranberry sauce, rinse it and allow to dry on a paper towel. Roll the cranberry in sugar to coat. Make enough of these to garnish each crepe.

Putting it all together. Put a crepe on a flat plate, then spread the cranberry mixture in a thin layer on the crepe. Now take 1/4 cup of whipped filling and spread it evenly across the middle of the crepe, place the right side of the crepe in a fold over the filling, and also on the left side over to the center. Lightly pour honey over the crepe and top with the toasted pecans, a spoonful of the crepe filling then top with a cranberry. It's optional to sprinkle now with confectioners' sugar.

Amber Richards

Egg Veggie Strata

1 medium sweet red pepper, finely chopped
1 cup sliced baby Portobello mushrooms
1 medium red onion, finely chopped
1 medium zucchini, finely chopped
2 teaspoons olive oil
3 garlic cloves, minced
2 teaspoons fresh thyme or 1/2 teaspoon dried thyme
2 packages (5.3 ounces each) fresh goat cheese, crumbled
1-3/4 cups grated Parmesan cheese
1/2 teaspoon salt
1/4 teaspoon pepper
1 loaf day-old French bread, cubed
1/4 teaspoon ground nutmeg
6 eggs, lightly beaten
2 cups fat-free milk

Instructions
Sauté red pepper, onions, mushrooms and zucchini in oil until tender in a large skillet. Add thyme, salt & pepper and garlic then cook 1 more minute.

Take a 9X13 baking dish sprayed with non-stick spray and layer half of the bread cubes, sautéed vegetable mixture, goat and Parmesan cheese, then repeat.

Whisk in a small bowl the milk, nutmeg and eggs then pour over the top. Refrigerate, covered overnight.

Half an hour before baking, remove from the refrigerator and preheat oven to 350° F. Bake for 45 minutes, uncovered, until a knife inserted in the middle comes out clean. Remove from heat and allow to set for 10 minutes before cutting. Makes 12 servings.

County Fair Blue Ribbon Winning Cookbook

Mustard Potato Salad

1/4 cup Dijon mustard
2 pounds small red potatoes
1 cup mayonnaise
1/2 teaspoon salt
1/2 teaspoon pepper
1/4 teaspoon lime juice
1/2 to 3/4 cup chopped red onion
2 green onions with tops, sliced
2 garlic cloves, minced
3 tablespoons snipped fresh dill

Instructions
Boil potatoes in water about 25 minutes, until tender, then drain and cool.

In a bowl mix the remaining ingredients. Then cut potatoes into bite sized pieces and put in a large bowl, fold in the mayonnaise mixture and toss until everything is coated. Serve this dish warm and it makes enough for 8-10 people.

Orzo & Wild Rice Salad

2 c. water
1 c. orzo
½ c. wild rice
3 T. green onion, chopped
½ chopped red bell pepper
½ chopped yellow bell pepper
2 T. fresh basil
1 ear fresh corn, cooked & kernels cut from cob
½ t. sea salt
¼ t. pepper
2 T. white wine vinegar
2 T. fresh lemon juice
1 minced clove garlic
½ c. olive oil
1 ½ t. honey

1 t. Dijon mustard

Instructions
Boil wild rice in water, then reduce heat and simmer 30 minutes until rice is tender and water is absorbed.

Cook orzo according to instructions on the package. Drain and add this to the wild rice. Cover then chill in refrigerator.

In a bowl add peppers, corn, onion, salt & pepper and basil. In a separate bowl, whisk lemon juice, vinegar, olive oil, garlic, mustard and honey together, then add to the vegetables. Add this all to the chilled rice and orzo, then chill another 2 hours before serving. Serves 4-6 people.

Casseroles

Asparagus & Ham Casserole

4 hard-cooked eggs, peeled and chopped
1 cup cubed fully cooked ham
2 tablespoons quick-cooking tapioca
1 package (10 ounces) frozen cut asparagus or 1 pound fresh asparagus, 1/2-inch cuts
1/4 cup shredded process cheese (Velveeta)
2 tablespoons chopped green pepper
2 tablespoons chopped onion
1/2 cup half-and-half cream or evaporated milk
1 cup condensed cream of mushroom soup
1 tablespoon minced fresh parsley
1 tablespoon lemon juice

TOPPING:
1 cup soft bread crumbs
2 tablespoons melted butter

Instructions
Add 1/2 inch of water to a large saucepan and bring to a boil. Put in asparagus, cover and cook 3 minutes. Drain and instantly put asparagus into ice water, then drain and pat dry with clean paper towels.

Put the asparagus into a 2 1/2 quart baking dish along with the ham and eggs. Sprinkle tapioca over the top, then stir in the green pepper, onion, parsley and cheese.

In a separate bowl mix the soup, cream and lemon juice, then add to the above mixture and stir completely.

Combine the topping ingredients and place on top of the casserole. Bake at 375° F. uncovered for half an hour. Allow to set 10 minutes before cutting. Makes 4 servings.

Cheesy Polenta Casserole

4 cups water, divided
1 pound ground beef
1 cup yellow cornmeal
1 teaspoon salt
1 cup chopped onion
1/2 cup chopped green pepper
1/2 pound sliced fresh mushrooms
1 teaspoon each dried basil, oregano and dill weed
2 garlic cloves, minced
1 can (14-1/2 ounces) diced tomatoes, undrained
1 can (8 ounces) tomato sauce
Dash hot pepper sauce
1/4 cup grated Parmesan cheese
1-1/2 cups (6 ounces) shredded part-skim mozzarella cheese

Instructions
In a bowl (for the polenta), whisk 1 cup of water, cornmeal and salt until smooth. In a saucepan, bring the remaining water to boil, then add cornmeal mix, and bring to a boil for 3 minutes, stirring constantly. Reduce heat, cover and simmer 15 minutes. Then divide this into 2 greased 8 inch square baking pans. Refrigerate, covered for 1-1/2 hours.

Cook onion, green pepper, garlic and beef in a skillet over medium heat until meat is completely cooked, then drain. Stir in mushrooms, herbs, hot pepper sauce, tomatoes and tomato sauce, then bring to a boil. Reduce heat and simmer 20 minutes, uncovered.

Take 1 polenta out of refrigerator and loosen it from bottom and sides of the baking pan. Put it on a wax paper lined cookie sheet and set aside.

Place half of the meat mixture over the first baking pan of polenta. Add half the Parmesan and mozzarella cheese, then finish off with the reserved polenta (on the wax paper) and the meat mixture.

Bake at 350° F. covered, for 40 minutes. Remove from heat and sprinkle with remaining cheeses and bake another 5 minutes. Allow this to set for 10 minutes before serving. Makes enough for 6 people.

Cheese and Scrambled Egg Casserole

CHEESE SAUCE:

2 cups milk
2 tablespoons butter
7-1/2 teaspoons flour
1/2 teaspoon salt
1/8 teaspoon pepper
1 cup cubed process cheese (American or Velveeta)
1 cup cubed fully cooked ham
12 eggs, beaten
1 can (4 ounces) mushroom stems and pieces, drained
1/4 cup chopped green onions
3 tablespoons butter, melted

TOPPING:
2-1/4 cups soft bread crumbs
1/4 cup melted butter

Instructions
Melt butter in a large skillet for the cheese sauce, then stir in flour and cook 1 minute. Gradually add in milk, stirring constantly and bring to a boil for 1 or 2 minutes until it gets thick. Add the cheese, salt & pepper and stir until the cheese is melted, then set aside.

Sauté green onion and ham in 3 T. of butter until onion is soft, then add eggs and cook until eggs are set. Stir in cheese sauce and mushrooms.

Place this into a greased 9X13 inch baking pan, then combine topping ingredients and sprinkle over the egg mixture. Refrigerate, covered overnight.

Next day, uncover then bake at 350° F. 30 minutes. Serves 10-12 people.

Soups

Cheese Dumplings & Hearty Beef Stew

2 to 3 pounds beef stew meat, cut into 1-inch pieces
2 tablespoons canola oil
1/2 cup flour
1/2 teaspoon salt
1/2 teaspoon pepper
5 cups water
5 teaspoons beef bouillon granules
1 tablespoon browning sauce, optional
1/2 teaspoon onion salt
1/2 teaspoon garlic salt
1 medium onion, cut into wedges
1 can (14-1/2 ounces) cut green beans, drained
4 medium carrots, sliced

DUMPLINGS:
1 cup shredded cheddar cheese
2 cups biscuit/baking mix
2/3 cup milk

Instructions
Combine salt, pepper and flour in a re-sealable bag, then add beef a couple at a time and shake. Brown beef in a couple of batches in a Dutch oven. When all the beef is browned, add bouillon, onion salt, browning sauce (if you are using it), garlic salt and water then bring to a boil. Reduce the heat and simmer, covered for 1 hour.

Add onion and carrots, and simmer 15 more minutes, then add in green beans.

To make the dumplings; in a bowl mix the cheese and biscuit mix. Add enough milk to form a dough, then drop by large spoonfuls on top of the stew. Cover and cook another 12 minutes or so, without lifting the lid during this cooking time. It is done when a toothpick inserted in the middle of a dumpling, comes out clean. Makes 6-8 servings.

Homemade Barley & Chicken Soup

1 chicken (2 to 3 pounds), cut up
8 cups water
1-1/2 cups chopped carrots
1 cup chopped celery
1/2 cup medium pearl barley
1 bay leaf
1/2 teaspoon poultry seasoning
1/2 teaspoon pepper
1/2 teaspoon rubbed sage
1/2 cup chopped onion
1 teaspoon chicken bouillon granules
1 teaspoon salt, optional

Instructions
Cook chicken in water until chicken is no longer pink, in a large stockpot. Cool broth, then skim off fat. Allow the chicken to cool, then remove bones and cut the meat into small pieces and return to the stockpot.

Add the rest of the ingredients and bring to a boil. Reduce heat and simmer covered for 1 hour. Toss out bay leaf right before serving, makes enough for 5 people.

Chicken & Biscuit Soup

2/3 cup shortening
5 to 6 tablespoons milk
2 cups flour
1-1/4 teaspoons salt

SOUP:
1 cup cubed peeled potatoes
1 cup chopped sweet onion
2 celery ribs, chopped
2 tablespoons butter
2 medium carrots, chopped
1/2 cup all-purpose flour
1/2 teaspoon salt
1/4 teaspoon pepper
1 cup frozen petite peas
1 cup frozen corn
3 cans (14-1/2 ounces each) chicken broth
2 cups shredded cooked chicken

Instructions
Add salt and flour in a large bowl and mix, then cut in shortening until the texture of coarse crumbs. Slowly add milk, stirring gently with a fork until a dough is formed when pressed. Form into a flattened oval shape, wrap in plastic wrap and chill for 30 minutes or more.

Roll dough to 1/8 inch thick on a floured surface, then using a 2-1/2 inch round cutter, create 18 circles. Put on ungreased cookie sheets and bake at 425° for 10 minutes until nice and brown, then cool on a wire rack

To make the soup, heat butter in a Dutch oven, add onion, celery, carrots and potatoes then cook for 8 minutes until the onion is soft.

Add salt, pepper and flour gradually, whisking until it is thoroughly mixed. Bring to a boil, then reduce heat and simmer 10 minutes uncovered. When the potatoes are tender, add the rest of the ingredients and allow to simmer another 15 minutes. Serve with the pastries, makes 6 servings.

Creamy Cauliflower Soup

2 celery ribs, sliced
2 garlic cloves, minced
2 medium onions, chopped
2 medium carrots, grated
1/4 cup plus 6 tablespoons butter, divided
1 medium head cauliflower, chopped
5 cups chicken broth
1/4 cup minced fresh parsley
1/2 teaspoon dried tarragon
6 tablespoons all-purpose flour
1 cup milk
1/2 cup heavy whipping cream
1/4 cup sour cream
1 teaspoon salt
1 teaspoon coarsely ground pepper
1/2 teaspoon dried basil
 Fresh tarragon, optional for garnish

Instructions
Sauté carrots, onions, garlic and celery in 1/4 cup butter in a Dutch oven, until tender. Add broth, parsley, tarragon, basil, salt & pepper and cauliflower, then cover and simmer half an hour until the veggies are soft.

In another pan melt remaining butter, stir in the flour until smooth. Gradually add whipping cream and milk, then bring to a boil, stirring while cooking for 2 minutes. Add this to the Dutch oven cooking the vegetables, and cook 10 more minutes until it has thickened. Stir several times during the process. Remove from heat and add sour cream. Makes 8 servings.

County Fair Blue Ribbon Winning Cookbook

Cream of Parsnip Carrot Soup

4 c. chicken broth
8 c. chopped carrots
1 chopped onion
4 minced garlic cloves
2 c. buttermilk
2 T. sour cream
6 c. parsnips (peeled and cut up)
3 c. water
2 t. sugar
1 t. salt
1 t. horseradish
1 t. minced ginger
3 T. butter
Fresh dill for garnish

Instructions
Put water, broth, sugar, salt, carrots and parsnips in a Dutch oven and heat to a boil. Reduce the heat and cook, covered for 30 minutes until veggies are soft.

Sauté garlic, horseradish, ginger and onion in butter in a small skillet until tender, then add to the Dutch oven.

In smaller batches, puree the soup with a food processor until smooth, then return to the Dutch oven. Add buttermilk and heat without boiling. Serve with dill and sour cream if desired. Makes 12 servings.

Hearty Sausage Stew

1 cut up sweet red pepper
2 pounds (cut to 1 inch pieces) smoked Polish sausage
1 cut up green pepper
8 to 10 medium red potatoes, cut up
2 quartered white onions
1 pint heavy whipping cream
3 T. water
3 T. cornstarch
2 tsp. salt
1 tsp. pepper
1/3 c. canola oil
1 T. dried basil

Instructions
Put peppers, sausage, onions and potatoes in a large roasting pan and mix. Add basil, salt & pepper and oil then pour over and toss to cover the vegetables. Bake at 350° F. for 45 minutes, covered, stirring occasionally. Add cream, then bake another half hour, covered.

In a small bowl mix the water and cornstarch, add to the stew. Put the roasting pan on the stovetop and bring to a boil until stew has thickened, while stirring constantly. Makes 10 - 12 servings.

Swiss Onion Soup

1-1/2 cups water
7 tablespoons butter, divided
1-1/2 cups cubed day-old bread
3 large onions, quartered and thinly sliced
4-1/2 teaspoons chicken bouillon granules
1-3/4 cups milk, divided
1-1/2 cups (6 ounces) shredded Swiss cheese, divided

County Fair Blue Ribbon Winning Cookbook

1/4 cup all-purpose flour
Pepper to taste
Fresh minced chives

Instructions
Add to the bread cubes 3 T. of melted butter and toss lightly. Put this on a greased cookie sheet and bake at 350°F for 7 minutes, turn and bake another 7 minutes.

Sauté onions with the rest of the butter until tender, stir in bouillon and water then bring to a boil. Reduce heat and simmer 15 minutes, covered.

Mix 1/2 cup milk and flour until smooth, then slowly add to the onion mix and add the remaining milk. Bring this to a boil and cook for 2 minutes until thickened, stirring constantly. Remove from heat and add pepper and 3/4 cup Swiss cheese then stir until melted.

Spoon into 4 bowls that are ovenproof and sprinkle with the toasted bread crumbs and remaining cheese. Broil in the oven for a couple of minutes, close to the heat source until the cheese is bubbly, garnish with chives. Makes 4 servings.

Pumpkin Curry Soup

2 tablespoons butter
1/2 pound fresh mushrooms, sliced
1/2 cup chopped onion
2 tablespoons flour
1/2 to 1 teaspoon curry powder
3 cups vegetable broth
1 can (15 ounces) solid-pack pumpkin
1/2 teaspoon salt
1/4 teaspoon pepper
1/4 teaspoon ground nutmeg
1 can (12 ounces) evaporated milk
1 tablespoon honey

Minced chives

Instructions
Sauté onion and mushrooms in butter until soft. Add the curry powder and flour then stir well. Slowly add the broth and bring to a boil, cooking for 2 minutes until it has thickened, stirring constantly.

Add milk, honey, pumpkin, nutmeg, salt & pepper and allow to simmer until its heated all the way through. Garnish with chives. Makes 7 servings.

Healthy & Delicious Root Soup

3 parsnips
3 med. kohlrabi
2 lg. shallots1 lb. veal stew meat (cubed to bite-size)
1 lg, yam
5 or 6 cloves garlic
4 or 5 carrots
2 portabella mushrooms
6 or so small red potatoes
2 or 3 bay leaves
Olive and sesame oil
Salt and pepper
Apple cider
Chicken stock

Instructions
Cut into bite sized cubes the red potatoes, carrots, kohlrabi and parsnips. Put the oils in a stock pot, add the vegetables and stir to coat them. Transfer the vegetables to a roasting pan and roast at 450°F for 30 minutes, stir a couple of times during the roasting time. While these are roasting, cook the meat in the stock pot.

Sauté garlic and onion in some oil until tender then add the mushrooms. Add this now to the stock pot along with the roasted vegetables, bay leaves, salt & pepper, stock and cider. Cook for 15 minutes on medium heat. Ready to serve.

Bean & Ham Chowder

1 cup sliced celery
2 garlic cloves, minced
1 pound dried great northern beans
2 cups chopped onion
3 tablespoons butter
1 meaty ham bone
2 cups water
2 whole cloves
1/2 teaspoon pepper
2 cups milk
1 can (14-1/2 ounces) chicken broth
1 can (14-1/2 ounces) stewed tomatoes
2 bay leaves
2 cups shredded cheddar cheese

Instructions
In a soup kettle put in the beans and add water to cover them by 2 inches. Bring to a boil and boil 2 minutes, remove from heat, cover and set aside for 1 hour.

Drain beans while discarding liquid. Using the same soup kettle sauté celery, garlic and onion in the butter until soft. Add ham bone, water, beans, broth, tomatoes, pepper, cloves and bay leaves then bring to a boil. Reduce heat and simmer for 2 hours, covered.

Remove bay leaves, cloves and ham bone. When the ham bone is cool enough, remove the meat from the bone and put the pieces (cut up) back to the soup, discard the bone. Chill overnight, then skim fat from the top of the soup. Add milk and cook on low until heated. Right before serving, top with cheese. Makes 12-14 servings.

Amber Richards

Goulash Hungarian Style

4 medium onions, chopped
6 garlic cloves, minced
1-1/4 pounds beef stew meat, cut into 1-inch cubes
2 tablespoons olive oil, divided
2 teaspoons paprika
1/2 teaspoon caraway seeds, crushed
1/2 teaspoon pepper
1/4 teaspoon cayenne pepper
1 teaspoon salt, optional
2 cans (14-1/2 ounces each) reduced-sodium beef broth
2 cups cubed peeled potatoes
2 cans (28 ounces each) diced tomatoes, undrained
1 large sweet red pepper, chopped
2 cups sliced carrots
2 cups cubed peeled rutabagas
  Sour cream, optional

Instructions
Brown the beef in 1 T. of oil in a Dutch oven over medium heat. When cooked, remove the beef and drain, set aside. Heat the rest of the oil in the same Dutch oven and sauté onions until tender, then add garlic and continue cooking for another minute.

Add salt & pepper, cayenne, caraway and paprika, stirring for another minute. Put the beef back in, then add rutabagas, carrots, potatoes and broth then bring to a boil. Reduce the heat and simmer 1-1/2 hours, covered.

Add red pepper and tomatoes then bring to a boil. Reduce heat, simmer another 30 minutes, covered. Serve with sour cream, makes 15 servings.

County Fair Blue Ribbon Winning Cookbook

Spiced Shrimp Bisque

1 T. olive oil
2 minced garlic cloves
1 onion, chopped
1 T. flour
1 c. water
1/2 c. heavy whipping cream
1/2 t. ground coriander
1/2 pound peeled and deveined uncooked medium shrimp
1/2 c. sour cream
2 t. chicken bouillon granules
1 T. chili powder
1/2 t. ground cumin
Garnish with fresh cilantro and avocado, optional

Instructions
Sauté the onion in oil until tender in a saucepan, then add garlic and cook another minute. Add flour and stir, then add bouillon, water, seasonings and cream. Bring to a boil, then reduce the heat and simmer for 5 minutes, covered.

Add shrimp and simmer 10 minutes, until shrimp are pink. Put sour cream in a small separate bowl, and add 1/2 cup of the hot soup and stir until blended. Now fold this into the main pan of soup, stirring until thoroughly mixed, and heated, yet do not allow it to boil To serve, top with avocado and cilantro. Makes 3 portions.

Beefy Mushroom Stew

1 ounce dried mixed mushrooms
1/4 cup flour
1 carton (32 ounces) beef broth
1 teaspoon salt
1 teaspoon pepper
1 boneless beef chuck roast (2 pounds), cubed

3 tablespoons canola oil
1 pound whole baby Portobello mushrooms
3 garlic cloves, minced
3 teaspoons minced fresh rosemary or 1 teaspoon dried rosemary, crushed
5 medium carrots, chopped
1 large onion, chopped

ADDITIONAL INGREDIENTS:
2 tablespoons cold water
2 tablespoons cornstarch
1/4 cup crumbled blue cheese
Hot cooked egg noodles, or hot cooked rice optional

Instructions
Boil the dried mushrooms and broth in a large saucepan. Remove from heat and allow to sit for 20 minutes so mushrooms soften. Drain and reserve the liquid. Chop mushrooms and set apart.

In a re-sealable bag mix flour, salt & pepper. Reserve 1 T. of this for the sauce. Add the beef into the bag, several pieces at a time and shake to coat thoroughly. Brown the beef in batches in a Dutch oven with some oil.

When the beef is done, add carrots, onion and Portobello mushrooms then sauté until onion is soft. Add the re-hydrated mushrooms, rosemary and garlic, cooking 1 minute. Stir in the 1 T. of flour stirring well, and gradually add the mushroom broth, then heat to a boil. Reduce heat and simmer 2 hours covered.

Bring to a boil once more, mix water and cornstarch in a small cup and add to the stew gradually, and cook a couple of minutes, stirring constantly until it has thickened. If desired, serve over egg noodles or rice, and top with blue cheese. Makes 9 servings.

County Fair Blue Ribbon Winning Cookbook

Delicious Bean Soup

3 cups water
1 meaty ham bone or 2 smoked ham hocks
2 cups dried great northern beans
5 cups chicken broth
2 to 3 tablespoons chicken bouillon granules
1 teaspoon dried thyme
1/2 teaspoon dried marjoram
1/2 teaspoon pepper
3 medium carrots, chopped
3 celery ribs, chopped
1 tablespoon canola oil
1/4 teaspoon rubbed sage
1/4 teaspoon dried savory
2 medium onions, chopped

Instructions
Rinse beans with cold water and sort, tossing out any that look odd. Put in a soup kettle or Dutch oven and add enough water to cover the beans by 2 inches. Bring to a boil and cook 2 minutes. Remove from the heat, and allow to sit 4 hours, covered until beans are tender.

Drain then rinse the beans, discarding the liquid. Put the beans back in the soup kettle. Add 3 cups of water, broth, seasonings, bouillon and ham bone. Bring to a boil, the reduce heat and simmer 1 1/2 hours, covered.

Sauté celery, carrots and onions in oil in a large skillet until soft. Add this to the soup, simmer another hour, until beans are completely cooked.

Remove the ham bone and allow to cool until it can be handled. Remove the meat and cut into smaller pieces, then return back to the soup. Toss out the bone, then skim the fat off the soup. Makes 10 servings.

Amber Richards

Chili Pepperoni Pizza Style

1 can (16 ounces) kidney beans, rinsed and drained
1 can (15 ounces) pizza sauce
1 pound ground beef
1 can (14-1/2 ounces) Italian stewed tomatoes
1 can (8 ounces) tomato sauce
1/2 cup chopped green pepper
1 teaspoon pizza seasoning or Italian seasoning
1 teaspoon salt
1-1/2 cups water
1 package (3-1/2 ounces) sliced pepperoni
Shredded mozzarella cheese, optional

Instructions
Cook beef on medium heat in a large saucepan until fully cooked, then drain. Add pizza sauce, seasonings, salt, green pepper, pepperoni, water, tomato sauce, tomatoes and beans. Bring this to a boil, then reduce heat and simmer for 30 minutes, uncovered. Before serving, sprinkle with cheese. Makes 8 portions.

Sweet Bell Pepper Soup

2 medium onions, chopped
1 celery rib, chopped
4 garlic cloves, minced
6 medium sweet red bell peppers, chopped
2 medium carrots, chopped
1 tablespoon olive oil
1-1/2 teaspoons salt
1/4 teaspoon pepper
1/8 to 1/4 teaspoon cayenne pepper
2 cans (one 49-1/2 ounces, one 14-1/2 ounces) chicken broth
1/2 cup uncooked long grain rice
2 tablespoons minced fresh thyme or 2 teaspoons dried thyme

County Fair Blue Ribbon Winning Cookbook

1/8 to 1/4 teaspoon crushed red pepper flakes

Instructions
Sauté garlic, celery, onions, carrots and red peppers in oil until soft, in a soup kettle or Dutch oven.

Add the rice, broth, cayenne, thyme, salt & pepper, bringing to a boil. Reduce the heat and simmer 25 minutes, covered. Make sure the rice and vegetables are tender, if not, cook a bit longer.

Cool for half an hour, and in small batches, puree in a blender until smooth, then return to the soup kettle. Sprinkle in red pepper flakes and re-heat until soup is hot. Makes 10-12 portions.

Old Fashioned Bean Soup

1 meaty ham bone or 2 smoked ham hocks
8 cups water
1 large onion, chopped
1 pound dried great northern beans
3 celery ribs, diced
1 can (28 ounces) crushed tomatoes in puree
2 tablespoons brown sugar
2 medium carrots, shredded
Salt to taste
1/2 teaspoon pepper
1/2 teaspoon dried thyme
  1-1/2 cups finely shredded fresh spinach

Instructions
According to package directions, soak beans (usually overnight) in water. In a large Dutch oven, drain and rinse the beans and put inside, along with the water and ham bone, then bring to a boil. Reduce heat, and simmer for 1 1/2 hours, covered until the meat is cooked.

Remove the bone from the soup and cool. Cut meat from the bone and into smaller pieces. Toss out the bone. Add the meat, broth, thyme, salt & pepper, carrots, celery and onion to the soup. Cook, covered for an hour, until vegetables and beans are soft. Add brown sugar and tomatoes and cook another 15 minutes.   Right before serving, toss in the spinach. Makes 5 quarts.

Black Bean & Sweet Potato Chili

1 large onion, chopped
1 tablespoon olive oil
3 large sweet potatoes, peeled and cut into 1/2-inch cubes
2 tablespoons chili powder
3 garlic cloves, minced
1 teaspoon ground cumin
1/4 teaspoon cayenne pepper
2 tablespoons honey
1/2 teaspoon salt
1/4 teaspoon pepper
2 cans (15 ounces each) black beans, rinsed and drained
1 can (28 ounces) diced tomatoes, undrained
1/4 cup brewed coffee
 1/2 cup shredded Monterey Jack cheese

Instructions
Spray a Dutch oven with non-stick cooking spray and sauté onion and sweet potatoes in oil under tender. Add cayenne, cumin, garlic and chili powder and cook for 1 more minute. Add salt & pepper, honey, coffee, tomatoes and beans. Bring to a boil, then reduce heat and simmer for 35 minutes, covered. Before serving, sprinkle with cheese. Makes 8 portions.

Pasta & Turkey Soup

2 medium onions, chopped
2 garlic cloves, minced
1 cup uncooked small pasta shells
1 pound lean ground turkey
3 cans (14-1/2 ounces each) chicken broth
2 cans (15 ounces each) white kidney or cannellini beans, rinsed and drained
2 cans (14-1/2 ounces each) Italian stewed tomatoes
1 teaspoon pepper
1/4 teaspoon salt
1/4 teaspoon crushed red pepper flakes
2 teaspoons dried oregano
2 teaspoons dried basil
1 teaspoon fennel seed, crushed

Instructions
According to the package directions, cook the pasta. While it is cooking, in a large soup kettle, cook onions and turkey on medium heat until meat is thoroughly cooked. Add the garlic and cook another minute, then drain. Add seasonings, tomatoes, beans and broth, then bring to a boil. Reduce the heat and cook uncovered on low for 10 minutes.

Drain and rinse the pasta then add it to the soup, cooking 5 more minutes. Makes 10 portions.

Winter Hardy Beef Stew

2 T. flour
2 t. Montreal steak seasoning
2 pounds boneless beef sirloin steak (cut into 1 inch squares)
2 T. olive oil, divided
1 chopped onion
2 chopped celery ribs
1 can white kidney rinsed and drained (15 ounces)
1 can diced tomatoes, undrained (14-1/2 ounces)
1 c. dry red wine or beef broth
2 T. red currant jelly
2 parsnips, peeled and cut
2 peeled and cut carrots
2 minced garlic cloves
2 bay leaves
2 fresh oregano sprigs

Instructions
In a re-sealable plastic bag mix steak seasoning and flour, then add beef a few at a time and shake to coat. Brown the beef in a Dutch oven with 1 T. oil on all sides (in batches), then remove and keep warm.

In the same Dutch oven, sauté carrots, parsnips, celery and onion until tender, then add garlic and cook another minute. Add the beef back in, oregano, bay leaves, jelly, wine and tomatoes then bring to a boil.

Bake at 350°F in an oven, covered for a 1 1/2 hours. Add beans and continue baking another half hour. Remove from heat and discard oregano and bay leaves. Makes 8 portions.

County Fair Blue Ribbon Winning Cookbook

Other

Walnut & Blue Cheese Tart

1 refrigerated pie pastry
1/4 cup heavy whipping cream
1 egg
1 package (8 ounces) cream cheese, softened
1/3 cup crumbled blue cheese
1 garlic clove, minced
1/4 teaspoon cayenne pepper
1/4 teaspoon coarsely ground pepper
3 tablespoons chopped walnuts, toasted
2 tablespoons minced fresh parsley
1/3 cup chopped roasted sweet red peppers

Instructions
In an ungreased 9 inch fluted pie pan with a removable bottom, press the pasty to the bottom and up the sides, then trim the edges. Bake in a 425° F. oven for 9 minutes, until it is light brown, and cool on a wire rack.

Beat cream cheese, garlic and blue cheese in a bowl until blended. Add pepper, cayenne, egg and cream and beat until fully mixed. Spread this into the cooled crust, the top with parsley, walnuts and red peppers.

Bake at 375° F. for 20 minutes. Makes 12 portions.

Chicken Buffalo Dip

3/4 C. wing sauce (a hot sauce)
2 C mozzarella cheese
1 lb of chicken breast
8 oz cream cheese
3/4 C. ranch dressing
Celery (optional)

Instructions
Cut chicken into bite sized pieces, then cook in a skillet with salt and pepper. To a mixing bowl, whip the cream cheese, then add wing sauce and ranch dressing. Combine this with the chicken and 1 cup of cheese.

Pour this now into a baking dish and top with remaining cheese. Bake at 350° F. for 20 minutes. Serve with tortilla chips or celery.

Blue Cheese Dip

1/4 to 1/2 teaspoon salt
1 cup (4 ounces) crumbled blue cheese
1/3 cup minced chives
1 package (8 ounces) cream cheese, softened
1/3 cup sour cream
1/2 teaspoon white pepper
Apple and pear slices and/or toasted pecan halves

Instructions
With a mixer, beat sour cream, cream cheese, salt and pepper until well mixed. Add in the chives and blue cheese. This can be served with chips, pear or apple slices or any other item you wish to dip. Makes 1 3/4 cups of dip.

County Fair Blue Ribbon Winning Cookbook

Rhubarb Crepes

3 eggs
1/4 c. sugar
1/4 t. salt
1 c. flour
Additional butter
1 c. milk
5 T. melted butter

SAUCE/FILLING:
1 package softened cream cheese (8 ounces)
1 c. sugar
2 c. chopped rhubarb
Confectioners' sugar
1 T. cornstarch
1/4 t. ground cinnamon

Instructions
Whisk melted butter, sugar, salt, eggs and milk together in a large bowl. Add the flour and beat until smooth, allow to sit for 30 minutes.

In a non-stick skillet melt 1/2 tsp. butter and allow to heat. Put 1/4 cup of batter onto the pan, then lift the pan and swirl to spread it out. Cook until edges are light brown and the center is no longer fully liquid, gently turn it over and brown the other side. Put it on a plate and cover with a paper towel, and finish cooking the rest of the crepes.

To make the sauce, in a saucepan add sugar, cinnamon and cornstarch, then add the rhubarb. On medium heat, bring this to a boil, cooking for 2 minutes until it thickens, and the rhubarb is tender. Remove from heat and allow cool some.

Amber Richards

For the filling, mix 1/4 cup of rhubarb sauce and cream cheese until creamy. Place some of this on a crepe and fold in half, then fold in another half to make a triangle shape, or you can simply roll it, if you prefer. Top with a little sauce and dust with confections' sugar. Makes 10 servings.

Chicken Salad with Curry Sandwiches

2 teaspoons lemon juice
1 tablespoon chopped green onion
1 teaspoon curry powder
6 lettuce leaves
6 croissants, split
2 cups cubed cooked chicken breast
3/4 cup chopped apple
3/4 cup dried cranberries
3/4 cup mayonnaise
1/2 cup chopped walnuts
1/2 cup chopped celery

Instructions
Mix chicken, cranberries, mayonnaise, curry powder, onion, lemon juice, celery, walnuts and apple in a bowl. On the croissants, place lettuce leaves, then add the chicken salad on top. Makes 6 portions.

Soufflé Italian Style

1/4 c. chopped fine sweet bell pepper
6 egg whites
3/4 c. croutons
1 chopped l onion
2 ounces chopped thinly sliced prosciutto
2 t. olive oil
1-1/4 c. milk
1/4 t. cream of tartar
1/4 c.shredded Italian cheese blend

County Fair Blue Ribbon Winning Cookbook

1 egg yolk, lightly beaten
2 c. fresh spinach
1 minced garlic clove
1/3 c. flour
1/2 t. salt
1/4 t. pepper

Instructions
Allow egg whites to sit at room temperature in a large bowl for half an hour. Meanwhile process croutons in a food processor until ground into fine crumbs. Spread onto the bottom and up 1 inch of the sides of a greased soufflé dish.

Sauté red pepper, prosciutto and onion in oil in a large saucepan for 5 minutes until soft. Add garlic and spinach then cook until the spinach wilts. Stir in salt, pepper and flour, then gradually add milk. Bring to a boil and cook 2 minutes, stirring constantly, it will thicken a bit.

Move this to a large bowl, and add a little amount of this to the egg yolks, stir and transfer this back to the large bowl, constantly stirring. Allow to cool some.

Back to the egg whites, add the cream of tartar and beat with a mixer until stiff peaks form. Fold gently into the vegetables. Pour this mixture into the soufflé dish, and top with cheese.

Bake for 40 minutes in a 350°F oven, until top is puffy and the middle appears set. Remove from heat and serve. Makes 4 portions.

Cheese Spread Louisiana Style

1 teaspoon Worcestershire sauce
1/2 teaspoon prepared mustard
1 package (8 ounces) cream cheese, softened
1 tablespoon grated onion
1 cup finely chopped pecans, toasted
1 garlic clove, minced
1/4 cup butter, cubed

1/4 cup packed dark brown sugar
  Assorted chips or crackers

Instructions
Mix onion, garlic and cream cheese in a small bowl, then move to a serving plate, form into a 6 inch oval. Set this aside.

Combine brown sugar, butter, mustard and Worcestershire sauce in a small saucepan, cooking over medium heat 5 minutes, stirring. Remove from heat and add pecans. Allow this to cool, then place over cheese. Serve with chips or crackers. Makes 8 portions.

Special Chicken Salad

3 pounds boneless skinless chicken breast
1/2 teaspoons garlic powder (Not salt)
Salt and fresh ground pepper to taste
3 cups mayonnaise.
5 ribs celery, chopped save tops for poaching water for chicken
1 1/2 cups seedless green grapes cut in half.
1/2 teaspoons dried thyme

Instructions
Cook the chicken breast in water with parsley, onions, carrots and celery tops, until chicken is fully cooked. Remove from heat and cool, removing vegetables and celery tops. Cut chicken into small pieces.

Put the chicken, grapes and celery into a bowl, then add salt, pepper, garlic powder and thyme. Next add mayonnaise, using enough to make it creamy. Cover and chill at least an hour before serving. Makes 8 portions.

County Fair Blue Ribbon Winning Cookbook

Beef & Onion au Jus

1 garlic clove, minced
1 teaspoon browning sauce, optional
1 loaf French bread
1 cup shredded Swiss cheese
2 tablespoons canola oil
1 beef rump roast or bottom round roast (4 pounds)
2 large sweet onions, cut into 1/4-inch slices
6 tablespoons butter, softened, divided
5 cups water
1/2 cup soy sauce
1 envelope onion soup mix

Instructions
Over medium high heat in a Dutch oven, brown the roast on all sides in oil and then drain. Sauté onions in 2 T. of butter in a large skillet, until soft. Add soy sauce, soup mix, garlic, browning sauce (if using) and water, then pour over the roast.

Bake at 325° F. covered, for 2 1/2 hours. Remove from heat and allow meat to sit for 10 minutes before cutting. Slice into thin pieces and return to pan juices.

Cut the bread lengthwise and butter with remaining butter. Put on a cookie sheet and broil bread for 3 minutes until browned. Remove from heat and add onions, beef and top with cheese. Broil another 1 or 2 minutes until cheese is melted. Serve with the pan juices. Makes 12 portions.

Amber Richards

Corn Bread & Rhubarb Stuffing

5 cups chopped fresh or frozen rhubarb thawed
3 cups crushed corn bread stuffing
1/2 cup chopped walnuts
1/2 cup sugar
1 medium onion, chopped
1/2 cup butter, divided

Instructions
Toss sugar and rhubarb in a large bowl, then set apart. Sauté onion in 2 T. butter until soft, then add to the rhubarb. Add walnuts and stuffing.

Melt the rest of the butter in a skillet over medium heat and pour over the stuffing and toss lightly with a fork to blend.

Spoon this into a 2 quart greased shallow baking dish and bake at 325° F., uncovered for 40 minutes. Makes 6-8 servings.

Strawberry Crepes

1-1/4 cups flour
2 tablespoons sugar
Dash salt
1-1/2 cups milk
3 eggs
2 tablespoons butter, melted
1/2 teaspoon lemon extract

TOPPING:
2 tablespoons cornstarch
3/4 cup water
1/2 cup sugar
1 tablespoon lemon juice

1/4 teaspoon red food coloring, optional
4 cups sliced fresh strawberries
1 teaspoon strawberry extract

FILLING:
2 cups confectioners' sugar
1 teaspoon vanilla extract
1 cup heavy whipping cream
1 package (8 ounces) cream cheese, softened

Instructions
Mix the eggs, extract, butter and milk in a large bowl with a mixer. In a separate bowl mix the dry ingredients of sugar, salt and flour, then add to the milk combination and ensure it is well mixed. Chill for an hour, covered.

Heat an 8 inch, greased non-stick skillet over medium, add 2 - 3 T. of batter to the middle of the pan, then lift it up and swirl to spread batter into a larger circle. Cook until the middle no longer looks liquid, then carefully flip over and cook over side. The second side won't take as long to cook. Put on a wire rack to cool, adding paper towels between crepes.

Combine cornstarch and sugar in a small pan, then add lemon juice and water, stirring until smooth. Bring this to a boil, on medium heat, stirring for a minute, until it has thickened. Add food coloring (optional) and extract. Remove from heat and allow it to cool, then add the strawberries.

In a separate bowl, mix the cream until stiff peaks form, and set aside. In another bowl beat cream cheese, vanilla and confections' sugar until it is smooth, then gently fold in the whipped cream.

Take a crepe, and add 2 T. of filling in the center and spread it down the middle of the crepe, then roll it up. Add strawberry sauce on top. Makes about 20 crepes.

Amber Richards

Little Sausage Buns

1 cup chopped onion
1 can (16 ounces) sauerkraut, rinsed and well drained
1/2 pound Polish sausage, coarsely chopped
6 bacon strips, diced
2 tablespoons brown sugar
1/2 teaspoon garlic salt
1 package (16 ounces) hot roll mix
2 eggs
1/4 teaspoon caraway seeds
1/8 teaspoon pepper
1 cup warm water (120° to 130°)
Poppy seeds
2 tablespoons butter, softened

Instructions
Cook bacon in a skillet until done, then allow it to cool on paper towels, reserving 2 T. of drippings. In those drippings sauté the onion until soft. Add the sausage, sauerkraut, pepper, caraway, garlic salt and brown sugar and cook for 5 minutes, stirring. Remove from heat and add the bacon. Remove from heat and allow to cool.

Combine the ingredients for the roll mix and it's yeast packet in a large bowl. Stir in water, butter and 1 egg and stir to form a dough. Turn this out on a floured surface and knead about 5 minutes. Put this in a large bowl and cover with a clean towel and let it set for 5 minutes.

Divide the dough into sixteen sections. Roll out each one on a floured surface to a 4 inch circle. Put 1/4 cup of the filling on top of each one, then fold the dough around each, making a ball, then pinch the edges together to seal it. Put these, seam side down on cookie sheets that have been lightly greased. Take plastic wrap that has been lightly sprayed with cooking spray and loosely cover, allowing them to rise in a warm area for 15 minutes.

Whisk the remaining egg and brush the dough, sprinkle with poppy seeds to finish. Bake in a 350° F. oven for 15-18 minutes, until golden brown, Makes 16 portions.

Italian Sun-Dried Tomato Jam

1 garlic clove, minced
1 cup water
1 jar (7 ounces) oil-packed sun-dried tomatoes
1/2 medium onion, thinly sliced
1 teaspoon dried basil
1/2 teaspoon salt
1/2 teaspoon pepper
1/2 cup chicken stock
1/4 cup red wine vinegar
1 tablespoon sugar

Instructions
Drain and finely chop the tomatoes and set aside 1 T. of the oil. Sauté in a large saucepan the oil, onion and tomatoes until soft. Add the garlic and cook another minute. Next add salt & pepper, basil, sugar, vinegar, stock and water, then bring to a boil. Reduce heat and simmer for half an hour, covered. Uncover, then simmer for 20 minutes until liquid has reduced and it has the texture of jam. Remove from heat and chill.

It is now either ready to serve, or can be refrigerated up to a week in an airtight container. Makes 1 1/2 cups. This is a wonderful spread on crackers too.

Conclusion - I hope you have enjoyed making some of these amazing foods. Look for other cookbooks in this series to come shortly and consider adding them to your collection.

If this cookbook has provided value to you in any way, would you be so kind as to leave a review on Amazon? Thank you!

Made in the USA
Middletown, DE
22 November 2015